T0367248

GROWING UP

GROWING UP

GROWING UP

JEANNIE LYNN

GROWING UP

iUniverse books may be ordered through booksellers or by contacting:

iUniverse
1663 Liberty Drive
Bloomington, IN 47403
www.iuniverse.com
1-800-Authors (1-800-288-4677)

ISBN: 978-1-5320-5687-1 (sc)
ISBN: 978-1-5320-5688-8 (e)

Library of Congress Control Number: 2018910446

Print information available on the last page.

iUniverse rev. date: 08/31/2018

CONTENTS

1

(GROWING UP.) BY JEANNIE LYNN

From What I heard from my Family Members and Listening and Living!

Children being born into and growing up with a family of drinking have a hard life. Neglect. Physical and sexual abuse a daily issue in my childhood. Luckily there were some caring adults in my life. Dad was in the Army and Mom stayed at her mom's. Went mom had Mae her 1st born with dad she gives her to Grandma W. To care for; them dad and Mom was married. After he was out of the Army 1945, Parents who go out to bar's and have people in our home for beer parties. Sis. was dad 2sd. born child that we know she was born in a shack in the woods near the levy a place called Cr Bar Holler. We all moved to Sabina before I was born my Dad who thought I was not his baby, had accused Mom of having an affair while drinking. Dad and Mom went out to the bar. Dad got drunk that night, and going home they started fighting about the baby, {which was me} mom was having and who it or I belong to. Dad wrecked the car wanting to; Kill Me before I was born. Our parents would take all of us kids with them to the bar in Baine, while they drink we ran in and out playing in the ally and in the street. Our Dad was very abuse when drinking. you will see more as you read the whole story.

Growing up with our parents was not easy for me or my sibling. Sis. and I would do the cooking. My other sisters would do the cleaning of the house. The boys would get the wood in and do the outside work. Learning to cook on an old wood cook stove was hard, but we learn for we weren't support to not play with fire. We needed it to cook for ourselves. We would kill chickens and clean them for our Sunday meal and Sis. and I would cook them.

We as children went through a lot of abuse. Dad would get drunk on whisky and try to get into bed with us girls. Dad had raped Sis. at a young age. Dad would whip us with what he could find like belts and beat us. He was very mean when he was drinking after coming home. Dad did work hard on a farm but what money he would make went on drinking. Dad did try to kill Mom Three times, ones when he burned the house, before Sis. was born. The 2nd. time and the wrack and on route 50 in a hay pile, because she was drinking with another man. There was a car go by and saw what was happing, they stopped and called the sheriff's office. They did come, and Dad was taken to jail.

We had a grandmother who taught us a lot about cooking and caring for ourselves. She would come up and care for us when Mom was in the hospital and Dad was in jail. This happen all the time one of them was always laid up. Mom was drinking she would hide her beer so no one else could drink it. There was this one-time Grandma came up and we didn't have a lot of food in the house, she half of beans and oats together. They tasted awful our dogs wouldn't eat them. Thank God for our grandma every day for saving my life and my sibling.

Letting people know growing up and being born to Alcoholic families is not easy. You can overcome this and not do what they did, learn from their mistakes. Learn to cook and cleaned. To survive I'm graceful I did. Keep your grandparents close by. Dealing with the abuse in our life was hard. No family member can touch you in a sexual or physical way. Learn right from wrong and how to survive.

Thank You God for I'm a Survivor, Report abuse; don't wait for it to happen to you. There will be a lot of stories in this book that will upset you, written by me and is true. Getting married is not all it's cut out to be. And if you have children's. My family went through lots of bull, raising children without a father who is out playing around. I hope you get a lot out of this book and see what life has in store for you.

I drink after all my kids was born and followed my mom's footsteps. Lat. you see what my marriage was like and now I'm an AA member 2001 you will read all of this and more learn from my mistakes and don't go that path. And yet today 2018 I'm 18 Year's sober. And feeling good.

I can't tell you a lot about my 2 sisters be for me. They were here before me and Dad and Mom Didn't speak of them a lot. But Dad did say sis wouldn't speck to anyone.

1940 Dad met Mom and went out for a while he was home for two weeks leave Dad and Mom made love and she got with a child by him, it was time for Dad to go to the base and they was ship out to Peral Harder he was a cook there and was away from the war part of this place. 1941 he came back home again Dad met with Mom he saw she was with a child their kid, but they made love before he was to go back to war. 1942 He went back and was not coming back before the baby was born he was going to be going till 1945, while Dad gone Mom had Mom's 1st, baby.

their baby their 1st born Mom could not care for her so she let dad mom have her to raise her. They name her, after both their mom's he was out they got married and started they're family.

Dad and Mom had her while Dad was in the Army (1941 tell 45,) she lives with my Grandma, And, Mom live with her mom Grandma, Mom could not care for her at the time. In 45 dad and mom got married and started their lives together. Our Grandma. on side Dad live near the levy where dad was born, and she live with grandma that was DAD and Mom live until they moved.

There, and dad got the small house back in the woods of a Holler just of Road near the levy, and their Sis was born in the 2-room house and there where dad try to burn the house down wanting to hurt Mom and Sis, why Mom drink a lot and ran around with who would buy the beer and have affairs with them. Dad worked on one a farm for the jakes and worked didn't make a lot of money. The jakes did give a hog, chickens, and milk for us to have.

Dad move form a Holler to Bainbridge. To work on a big farm for a Halt there for more money and Mom started drinking then and Dad left her alone a lot, so a young man would come around and drink with her. That was ok with Dad until Mom started to have affairs with then.

We all moved to Sabina, before I was born. Dad who thought I was not his baby. I would like to go back there now and see where I was born. Mom was twenty- six then.

2

(THIS STORY IS ABOUT ME AND HOW WE GROW UP!) JEANNIE LYNN

Remember I wasn't here yet all head by my Grandmothers.

I was born in (Sabina,) number 3 child And as I say mom did a lot of drinking and went out with a lot of guys who would buy. So, when mom had, my Dad was mad accursed her and I was not his baby so one night they went out drinking and started to fight about it and wrack the car wanting to kill me and mom. Dad said I was not his baby put he will take care of me. When I was born in October I was Blue Baby and Doctor Gave me up for dead, but my Grandma. didn't. She washes me and warp me up and got one of mom dish pans put blanket in it and put me on the of a wood cook stove oven door to warm me up. The Doctor said if I make it I would not live pass age 12, and I would have a lot of health problems growing up, and I did. Today Thank You Grandma for my Life. I live now despite what daddy wanted dad did do a lot for me when I get sick dad was the one there to care for eleven those I was not his baby. I was a lot of trouble growing up as a kid. When I get hurt I cry so hard and pass out.

We moved again after 2 years to Bainbridge, to the Wt. farm on out of town dad worked for them there and our car broke down and I got hurt and started to cry and couldn't stop and then I pass out, so dad ran with me to the doctor's office in Baine, the doctor couldn't find anything wrong with me, so doctor told dad what to do when that happen again. Put a wet cold rag on her head and that will bring her to. Mom did that a lot to so Dad know how to do this put there was time dad needed the Doctor. There where we pick black berries a lot for mom to make pies and to can them for the winter.

The farm had a full horse and he wanted someone to ride them, so we did, took them to the woods with use. There was this one dark black one that I liked, and I rode him and no one else could they all could not believe it. Sis. and I was left to care for the little one while they went out to the bars to drink we was only 3&4 age it was getting cold and there was no wood in the house so I saw dad cut wood with an Ax so I went out to cut some wood like he did so sis could build a fire and I cut my big toe sis raped it up good as she could when they came home dad took me to the hospital in Chilly For stiches. After that all we had to do was bring it in here there was always wood.

We move around a lot this time up Jester hill, and behind us was someone else who had pony's and horses that needed someone to ride then he saw there was a lot of us kids, so he came down to talk to dad and mom about letting us to riding then. Dad and Mom talked about it and say yes, we can, mom know who he was they had met before I was born. There where we got to do a rodeo, on the camp site place. We did barrel riding and calf roping. The horse walking was much fun too. This was the most fun place we lived. Next door to our home was the young boy he had a tree house in the tree were our winder was, so we could talk back and forth, we went to school together as friends only. They moved away.

Growing up where Dad could find work Farming was all Dad know how to do. Mom talk Dad into letting her go work at the factory in Green to make extra cash. School was about to start again, and Mom wanted use to have new things to wear. Mom got a ride to work and from work put on Friday nights she stops of in Bainbridge to drink and she find a way home. We live behind the high school then Lect. place at the time. this was an old house and dad let me drive. So, I could drive the trucker for the hay wagon and help in the fields Lect. need all the help he could get at this time.

Our parents went out to the bars quit often and left us all here at home alone. Mom 4 child was born, and thing got no better Mom was always in the hospital for care.

Then Mom child 5 was born, and we all played and help mom with cooking and the house cleaning. Here on this farm this man had some horses and we could ride them, and this one day we went black berry picking and took the horses back in the woods. I feel of and got hurt when dad got home he come got me and rushed me to the doctor's office again I had pass out and by the time dad got me there I woke up and look at him.

Then Mom child six was born, and thing was getting a bit better dad and mom still drank but not as mush we were having money problems. Dad work hard to keep a roof over our heads and food on the table, we had a lot of good friends who would bring thing to us from churches and Mom had someone pick us kids up for Sunday school. Winder was coming on and we didn't have wood for a fire and dad and mom went out leaving us home and cold, so I went out to find some wood and I saw dad us the axes and I tried to but cut my toe almost off sis work on it and couldn't get it to stop bleeding, by this time I needed more help so sis went next door for help they came and took me to hospital to sew my toe back on. On our way home, we stop in Baine at the bar and find them having a good time our next-door friend was not happy about that. Dad did get a good running car the man he worked for help.

Then Mom 7 first, boy was born, dad was so proud he got a boy, and then Then came Mom 8 child was a Boy born now dad has 2 boys. The drinking slowed up they didn't have the money to drink with, but mom still got drank.

There was man coming to our home and would bring beer with then and mom would go out with them to where we did not know. We were all still small Mom whet to a feed mill a got some sheep nipple to put on beer bottles for us to suck because we would brake our good baby bottles. Mom left our oldest sister to watch us one night and she tides us up to keep us in bed, so we wouldn't get hurt.

It was time for Sis. to start school in Baine at the young age. She went and would not talk to anyone at the school for a year, so they failed her. So, at the age of 5 I had to go to school so Sis. Wouldn't be alone. She did start talking after she saw me talk to them and she was afraid to play outside for she didn't know anyone there. I was so happy to be there

Be in school for I had other kids to play with and Sis saw this, so she joins us and got to enjoy playing. At the end of school year Sis. got pass put I didn't because of my age but I was 6 / 5 Bate, started, and she was shy, so I was with her in school. She stays shy for some time, but we stay together a lot until I got pass to the first grated and she got held back. But I still saw her, and she look that she was doing well so I didn't approach her. School for me was cool I got to go somewhere and see other people. I loved School.

Living here was fun at times and when we were left alone we would play in the house and this one time we were jumping from a stair way on to some pillars in the floor and someone with a gun shot in the window and hit one of us in the leg, dad and mom was not home they was at the bar. The cops were call by our next-door friend they came out and looked around took her to the Doctors in town, and then they went looking for our parents at the bar.

The next day the welfare department was call and came out to see all of us. They look around in the cabinets for food and to see if we had what we needed because they got complains about us. They wanted to know how they get money to drink on and can't buy food for the house and pay your bills. Dad wasn't home from work yet, so mom couldn't anther the Question, Mom did tell them we get from his work 2 milk cow for milk, and 1 hog for meat and we have 25 hens for eggs. Mom couldn't tell them mush more because she didn't know why they was there for so after they look around and saw nothing wrong they left. One Sunday we all took a walk back in the woods cause Dad wanted to talk to all of us, Dad wanted to move again and work for the Jake near the levy, so we all agreed.

Now we are moving in the house where Dad was born, and his Mom lived on and where dad he was born, this was a nice place lot of room an up-stair bedroom for all kids we all change schools, and this is where Gaye start to school. here is woods we can play in and thing we can do here Mom wanted a Garden, so we got one to work in and dad went to get some seeds to put in it and Mr. Jake gave us some corn seed.

We got 2 milk cows and chickens and 3 hogs to rise for food. Mom would order baby chick out of a catalog each year for fryer to kill for the freezer. Jake paid for the chick's mom ordered which was part of the meat package dad got for working. Mom raised a big garden we eat out of and we caned and freeze a lot. That what we did every year for food we all like wide greens and we all go out picking them and picking black berries for pies was nice I think we eat more then we picked.

The outhouse was way up on the hill and there was wild cats and panthers running lose so Dad would go up there with us carrying his gun he hunts with to make true we all got back to the house safe. During the day we all like going to the woods put Dad didn't think we should because of the wide animal wondering around. So, we listened and didn't go to the woods.

Later Sis. and I went to go to the outhouse and there Stood a black panther looking at us we back up to the house and got our self in side and told Dad. He at the outhouse. Dad got his gun and went out to fine him put he was gone, so dad kept the gun by the door and said to all of use no one outside he bought a bucket in the house if you need to go here this was the. And this was where we lived We believed there was more than 1 of them living in our woods we wear come up missing a full chicken. We didn't lock them in at night until we started missing them.

Now the off-owing year Fenny started school and she was ok with it put we all stayed closed together we went to School then and this is where we stayed for a while.

We would have fried chicken and black berry pies for our Sunday dinner. Dad would pick 3 chickens from the hen house and cut their heads of and let then hang a while Mom was heating up the water we would clean then, so we all started to pick then clean then Dad burned then to get the hair of then and Mom did the cutting then up. Our Sunday dinner was the best meal of the week.

Sis and I would help with Cooking, Mom show me how to make pie crust to make the pies. Me and my sisters learn a lot about cooking just watching mom and dad cook. I wanted to learn all I could. Why Mom was always sick, and Dad was always in Jail and that left no one here to help use. So, Sis and I learn what we could.

Dad and Mom would have people in our home for beer party's and lot of them got drunk, so we kids would stay outside and play we did not go in the house when they would be drinking.

The time there would take use with the to the bars because they weren't allowed to leave use by ourselves I learned how to do the tap dance on the bar. IN Town we were outside lot of the time and the Cop there was nice he knows who we were. So, he was taking all of us to the school playground play.

The Cop stayed there with use for a while and he had someone come down to the playground to watch use. Then he went back to work. Hind did go to the bar and let dad and mom know where we were at. Dad assured Hind that they were leaving soon. Dad came to the school and got use, and we all went home.

The next day was our Sunday dinner and mom had already started drinking and Dad was mad about something we didn't think it was dinner because dad know me, and my sister could cook it. So, we got the dinner on and we all eat dinner mom didn't eat she was drunk. So, after we all went out to play and Dad and Mom was fighting about what we don't know, now Mom is going out the driveway and Dad gets her a buts in the hay pile and sets it on fire trying to burn her to death. We kids was not much help put we tried to get her to of the fire, and a passerby saw what was happening and called the cops and then someone took Mom to the hospital then the cop took dad to jail.

The people who stop to help use when and got our grandma to stay with use. Dad did a week in jail and mom was out in 3 days, and again the welfare dept. Was called to invest as to what was going on. We did not know they was coming out, so they surprise us there was no food in the house was a mass not clean put we all was in school. so, the social worker gives mom list of places to get food close and another helpful thing to help us.

Mom was afraid to tell Dad about it because he doesn't want Charity handouts. Mom did go see the people about the food and bought home 5 boxes of food, and clothes for all of us. Then mom got food stamps to buy food with. Dad did not say much after that.

There was not a lot of food in the house, so grandma did the best she could grandma found a full bean and some acts and cook it together. But we left a mess under the table for her to clean up. Later Mom and Dad was back home then some of dad drinking buttes stop by and dad got drunk again on whisky and Mom was drunk and in bed like dead sleep. Sorry Grandma.

We all went upstairs to go to bed the boys slept on the side of the door and we all slept on the other side of the room and my sister was going to put me under the bed, so dad couldn't get to me, dad had already had Sis. and well know that. My other sisters got under there bed got under there bed willy were trying to get the light on the finely did. Dad came up and lifted the door of our room and went back down so we thought well he not going to come up here well we were wrong he tried to, but the boys stop him from doing that, they put their bed over the door. So, the boys left their bed there all night, so dad would not try again we all when to sleep.

My sister has always protected of me from harm she watches out for me, no one dear hit me, because I would still pass out when I'm hurt. We all were playing under a table and Will pulled the blanket and the table came over and hit my head a cut me open again I was pass out. Someone took me to the hospital and they kept me over night. Dad didn't want to do that because we did not have the money for the stay. The next day Dad and Mom continue to have their drinking friends over because they bring the beer to drink on and bring hotdogs and bread and other food to eat, so us kids would have food.

Someone went to Bonville and all the town, got together and put five big grin Trucks in our drive way with food toys clothes and a lot more thing three weeks before Christmas day. And after this thing was delivered three days before Christmas something bad happen our animal all died and the Tree we had up for Christmas Dance in to the middle of the room and we found all then going Why we still did not know. Put this was a good and bad year we had.

Dad lost his job, so we were getting ready to move. Put before this dad had one more party with their friends with food. Cook out the family came to our house there was 2 young boys and their father, then full more people came for this cook out, by this time I was ten age, I met Jay a nice boy we were the same age as me, so we set on the log to talk with me. We walked up in the woods he got a bother with him Lee, but I didn't talk with him I like Jay. There was a lot of boys come down from Hills' Roe H. was one of them I did go with him and he know I was too young, Jay and his family didn't come down much anymore. So, I didn't see him. My former boyfriend was a bit older than me.

Form here we move to Dill Rd. back of the high school behind here was a gravel pit we all played a lot this is ware Dad worked for Lect. again this is being I learn to Drive a Car at the age of ten. Dad and Mom went to Baine still to drink and play bowling with the Josh. family and Hind were watching use going in and out of the bar.

So, Hill stopped dad and ask him if he should be driving, Henny thought not so He know I learned to drive so Hill follow me to the bridge on 50, so I took use all home. This is being we all had a lot of fun and when our family has people in for beer parties as long they brought the drinks Mom Got so she was hide beer. Jay and Lee came over thought the Creek and up the long lane to see all of use. They lived on Hill Rd. I was still seeing an old boyfriend at the time and wasn't wanting anyone else. Later I found out that my former boyfriend was with someone in Baine then he came down home and want to be with me, he smells bad and drunk, so I brook up with him that night told him if you want a sucker go for it. by this time I'm fourteen. I didn't go out with any one for two years.

Lee and Jay s came over the creek up to our house then Lee ask me if I wanted to go with him, I said I need to think about that. so I did go out with him I was fifteen at this time he got me roses and a baby doll gown and pink dress. Lee got me some nice thing, he wanted me to meet his mother and wear the dress went to the movies a lot in Greens to the drive-in mom and dad trust him more than the others I went with.

Lee was working on a farm in Bainbridge and at lunch time I go to the bar where he was eating and he by me lunch after he take me back to the school we did this 3 day out of the week. Lee is a bit on the jealousy side done want anyone to talk to me thing went on as usably and we got closer, I continue to go to school. Lee would pick me up at our bus stop and take me to, so he could be with me. He went to work about same time as he works.

I had one teacher who didn't care for this she wanted to be to ride the bus, and at lunch time he would come get me to have dinner with him. My teacher saw this, so she sent a note home with sis. We have chilly soup and a hamburger, and then take me back to school. My teacher didn't want me doing that. So, I quit going up town and waited for Lee to come to the house.

As time pass by some where I feel in love with him. My love for him was real honest and true. But other boys form Knocker Stiffer would come around and Lee would get mad at me thinking I wanted them. by this time I'm in the 8th, grade worked hard to go to the 9th, grade. We moved again to a big house on filthy and I. back of the two school there, the Knocker Stiffer boys all came over to our home every week ends and brought beer for Mom, so they could be with all of us.

There is six of us girls in this home. Roe came back after six months wanting to take me out and I said no I'm seeing someone else. By this time, I was seeing Lee. We all moved again down on Route fitly an there were I'm going with Lee, I know Lee sister Lou long before we got Married then while we were going together we go there a lot and listen to records. I always like going to Lou 's to me that's was my best place to hang out.

Dad needed to sign papers for this. I'm still in School. Put the year of my birthday I want to get married and not go back to school. So, mom and dad said I'm losing my best cook. I was already with a child. I was with my 1st. child.

My wedding, Month before going back to school I quit and month before I was eighteen.

3

THE MARRIAGE AUGUST OF 68 ON A SATURDAY NIGHT AT 10PM.

My wedding day was Saturday in August. He was going to pick me up at noon to go get married, but he did not show up I had a beautiful dress on. I had my hair fixed up and, Sis, did my makeup for this day. I waited, and time was going by fast, we were going to the preacher house at 1; pm. Because we were going to go out somewhere after the wedding. To a dinner and movie in greenfield Thing did not tune out that way, Lee was late for his own wedding. I had already went to bed and he shod up at 10; pm and want to go get married he was drunk and blowing his horn and heling you ready to go. Being 9 hours late I ask him why, he said I was up to Beth all this time, yes, he said

So, I put my blue jean on and t-shirt we went to get married, and Jay his brother was with us, after we got married he give $5. To the preacher. And he gives it back to me we then went to get some beer to drink and he know I could not drink a lot, I would full of to sleep so we went back to mom place and was what I thought we go to bed and sleep.

So, Lee said you can go to bed I'm going to drink so sitter was upsetting by the stove, and I saw him kiss her which was more then I got. And my sitter was up to. Then when I found out he a cheater and would go out with anyone, I wanted to stay awake put I could not, so I went to sleep. Put I know Lee was going to be together with my sitter on our night. But they thought I couldn't see them and my sitter took her close of and they were kissing her. Behind the stove I saw this, Lee denied it what I seen. Lee got in bed with me, but I rolled over to sleep at this time the disbelieve and truth started 1st my mistake.

Later we stayed with his mother, he was working at the Packing Co. in Greenfield, Making good money so me and Lee and mom went out to shopping at yard sales to fill up a box of thing we need for new house his Mom and I went shopping one day she got use a full new things for our new apt. and when we got home he was there and ask me where have you been with your Mom, got out of the car to and we got a hand full of the things we both then Lee slapped me that didn't make his mom happy at all.

So, she put down the things and got a stich of the tree and took him running around the house. Don't you hit her again ! What I would do to see a replay of that again, we did go out to the Bars with his Mom and step DAD, Mom would slip me drink under the table. I wasn't at drinking age.

We would Dance and have fun me and my mother in law was close I cared for her as she did for me. Ida did tell me Lee was going to be like is Dad and run around with other women. But I already found that out. The night we got married.

Two week, into this married life, Lee come home and said I found us a 2-room apartment in Green I made an appointment with the landlord to see this on Saturday, Lee had already seen it. He was telling me all about it, we had to share the bath room, he want me to see it so Lee mom came there with use to look at the apartments, so I like it, so we took it and move there the following Saturday, we want back to Ida place to gathers thing up we needed to move in this 2 rooms it was furnished with bed and appliances the rent was $80. A month, by this time I was 3-month with my 1st. baby. thing was going well until I wanted to get out and walk around town my doctors said walking was good for me.

There was a dairy green next to use and I was wanting ice a lot, so I go there and get me some. Put I was binge watched ! I got to know the town well I met a friend who live in the 3 room apartments down stairs her name is Silly and Dab, Lee got to know then and shily and I started walking together as time pass it was almost time for Thanksgiving Day The greenfield paper had an ad in it to win a Turkey then I fill out all the ads and walk then all out to drop in the boxes. It came time for the drawing name for the turkey, my name was draw for one of the turkeys, my picture was in the paper and they ask me to do you know how to cook it, I said no I don't know how to cook it.

So, we took my turkey down to my mother in law for thanksgiving went to help her get dinner we had a good day, now it time for Christmas and we spent it with his mom I help her cook she is teaching me a lot about cooking, and I'm learning.

Silly and Dab are moving out of the 3 room apartments and I wanted it, so I went an asked our landlord about it. It rent for $125. month we need a bigger place before baby was born so we got it, I paid our rent Lee gave me the money to pay the bills, he was happy about the move it wasn't furniture, so we need to buy thing, for 3 rooms. There was this furniture store up the street form use I walk there to look at a full thing we need they had some use thing and was cheaper to buy. We got the thing on a payment plan, and I made sure all our bills got paid.

Sis. came to my home to help me with thing two months before Sam was born. Cause Lee didn't want me to be alone, so Sis came up a lot, Lee had a friend who came around who wanted to meet Sis one Friday night, I planned a dinner and Lee had his friend come over, so they could meet, we all set down to eat dinner, Sis. like what she seen. Ros like Sis, they went out together to get to know each other. Sis saw a lot of Ros after that Ros is a married man and Lee know this, I was over to my landlord place Baking a Cup cake and I came back to our place and Sis and Ros was having love in our bed.

I went back to her place to check on the cupcake and got then out of the oven I started back to our place and Ros was going Lee saw me coming back from her place, he saw that someone had sex on our bed and My sitter didn't clean up our bed after they use it. Lee went filling the bed and found a spot on it. He asks me I said Sis and Ros was having sex in it, but he did not believe me, so he accused me and roes of doing this. I denied it put he had is mine made up and nothing I said mattered.

I told Sis what he had accrued me of and after that Sis and Ros were go somewhere else to have sex, she didn't tell him that it was her and Ros in our bed. I told them they are not doing it here anymore. Sis never told Lee and Ros didn't either tell what they did. after it time I went out and started to walk a lot more, but I was home to get dinner for use win Lee got home from work. It seems I just wanted away from the house, I'd go to my appointments with the doctors I talked to people on the street and get accused of wanting then. it now getting close to having my baby and I was getting fed-up with all the accusing of wanting someone else.

We went to Bainbridge to get grocers at the store there we went down all the cuvee and hills he drives fast I was getting sick three week before the baby due so he took me to my grandma they in town and left me, grandma took me to a yard sale to get some clean thing to wear there all day and night, he was out with my sisters on copper mountain drinking up the food money and having the time of the life cheating on me, and he accuse me. He did come back the next day to get me and we went home with no food for the house. Why he spent the money on beer and a good time with my sisters.

Where was you he said at his mom and later I found out that was a lie, he was laying with my sisters and having sex.

I walked to the hospital May in I finely went in labor for our baby and Lee was late getting to the hospital for are 1st born it a boy and I name him Sam he didn't like the name put I did. Lee said he was at work I understood that put when he got to the hospital he was drunk. I already had our baby without him we went home form the hospital, Lee said he had the rest of the week of, we when down to his mom's alt that week and she help me with the baby working with to learn what I need to do.

I got my Driver's license after we moved from greenfield, so I could take Sam to doctors and get foods we need because he was always going. But after I did I was accused yet again for wanting to go out with other men. (I was told thought who do it will accuse you of doing what they do.) by his Mom.

Then when the next week started he got up to go to work put came home late. I had dinner on and he was mad at me why I didn't know. He finely told me he was looking for work, he said they HIRD me last week. Two weeks after his birth, our rent was paid for the month of May to the end of the month. I tried to work with him to understand what was going on noting I did or say was never right as he said it my fault, when the land lord found out he wasn't working we was ack to move out and we had no were to go, so we went to his moms again was not what I wanted to do. He found a small two room house in Knockemstiff.

Lee dad got this one for use and him dos lived in front of us, Lee still is drinking a lot, got this one for use and the rent was $35. month there was no water and no bath rooms like we had.

Lee and his brother and cousins went out drinking all the time we couldn't by food put he could get drunk. One night they all went out stilling thing that was not there, they got a stroller, bar bells and full another thing. Someone saw then taking there thing and Rod his dad was no better he got the stroller and hid it in the woods they but the bar bells in the well. The cop found 3 pieces of the stolen Item and the boys wasn't there they were at friends place.

The cops went looking for then at the bar seen then at the place behind the bar. all 3 of then went to jail and we had no money to pay there find, so there set it out for 10 days. Now after they got out of jail his Dad got some beer and then went to this town, to get a full black woman to have fun with all the boys was they and Rod was pocking then and Lee and Jay were using a bloom stick on then and burned their clothes. Lee Dad haul them all back to this town, were they lived. With me and Sam at the house.

Now Lee can't come up with the rent of $35. Or pay the Electric. bill. The land lord gave us another month put we need to come up with the rent or start packing our thing to move. Bud told Lee about this house behind them on the hill back in the woods like, so he went and look at it, the rent was FREE that all he needed to here because we didn't have money to pay with anyway. Lee came and told me were moving and I said where your see.

Now we are moving I didn't get to see this place until we were moving there. This run-down house had holds you could though RATS though and I did. Well it was time for bed and I put Sam down in his baby bed and give him a bottle, and a rat came in and got in is bed and was licking him. So, I put him in bed with me after that, and I covered up our head to sleep and rats was running across the bed. I feel then on top of use. I was afraid of them I heard they eat people when their hunger they were big ones.

Lee got up and got his gun to shoot them put they was gone. We had very little food to eat, I tried to make little as posable to starch what we had. Lee got out and shoot rabbits to eat for food and he sold some to get milk for baby. Now winter was setting in and it was getting cold, no wood to burn and no food so what was I to do rats crawling all over. We've been here now for 6 months in, now it November it was time for Thanksgiving and Lee family hadn't herd form use so they came over the hill coming up was slick, so they walk up. And found use without food out of everything. it was cold me and baby was covered up trying to stay warm.

Snow up here was heavy we eat a lot of snow cream. We had mush else to eat, Lee Mom and step Dad brother came up to see how we was. I was walking back though the field and his mom saw me and though I was a ghost. I was wearing he big boots & skies muck and big coat to keep warm, When Ida and Bud got to the house.

She saw how we was living and she got use off the hill. I didn't have a pair of shoes no socks on or a warm coat. I put on what I could find and then dress Sam for the trip. His bother took Sam of the hill and Lee load up the car we had to take a full of our clothes and thing we needed. Ida and Lee went down the hill and I was still trying to get down, my hands and feet was so cold Lee did finely come back up to get me down he put his glove on my hands he help me on down the hill. so we went to live with Ida and Bud.

Went we got there she helps me with my frost bit hands and feet. Ida kept than raped up until they get better. I couldn't stand these hurting hands and feet it was hard to walk. I couldn't wash Sam diapers my hands hurt so bad, so Ida wash then for me. It took four weeks for me to get back in shape to do anything.

Now it time for Thanksgiving dinner and I help her get dinner we all eat all the Family was down for pies. After November was gone by and December she took use to the Aids Dept, to get help for our Housing and food. We left a lot of our thing on the hill. Lee's dad moved in this house and took most of what we left, it was all junk anywhere. After we went to the welfare dept, we started to look for a house, we found one on the same road Ida lives' on. Down under the hill form them, Bob owned it one it a nice little 3 room house with a bath room. For $125. Month. Ida took care of the 1st month rent for use. We had the house and me and Ida cleaned it up, we furfure it with what people give use. We got a lot of new and use things but now we have a home again. We got a small heating stove for $50. So, we got started all over again.

Bob was talking to Lee about fixing the bathroom he did know what day Bob was coming over, he wanted him to help him fix the bathroom, so he left, leaving me alone with him. I let Bob in to fix the bathroom, so why not. This was Bob House and I didn't have anything to fear. He wants Lee to help him with the bath room.

Sam was a baby and I was watching my soaps on ch.6 he came home after being up his mom's, I told him Bob said he'll be back tomorrow to finely the job. He said he was going to get a full thing to fix the bathroom. Because he didn't get done, the 1st day Lee ask me if Bob took me to bed. I said no he did not, are you going to start that again.

He's mom told him you can't Trust bob he will try to bother her. That all he needed to hear to start accusing me again, because he was coming back to work on the bathroom, Lee thinks he's coming to be with me. Now he gone out again with the boys and drink, so knowing Bob would be here working on the bathroom/ Lee thought he was coming to be with me, I'm in the Kitchen washing dished and getting supper and bob was in the bathroom working on it.

He said I don't trust him, I got it feeling Lee didn't trust me, we finely got our welfare check medicated food stamps. Bob know how hard we were having things, so he asks if there was anything I can help you all with. So, I said yes, we need food furniture clothes and full other things. Then the follow Sunday we got all kinds of help, Lee accuse me of having sex with Bob to get this help. But I did not, I feel I don't have to sex with men to get what I want. We were here for 8 months.

(My thought why leaves the house if you know a man was coming you don't trust? If you don't trust the man fixing the Bathroom.)

Now he wants to move and get me away from Bob one who gave use so much help. I not ready to move again. Well we move to No Hill Rd. and old block house with and up stair in it and that were we sleep, now I'm with another child out number two.

When we move here I want to Start some flowers I ask Lee to bring down the dirt I had upstairs, so I can start planning them I had the pops and flowers ready to get started, He set there watching TV, I was waiting for him to go up and get that for me.

Remember I'm with a child, He never did go get the dirt, so I went up and got it myself. I started down with it and fell down the stairs carrying a 5-gallon bucket of dirt. Lifting for me got worse for me and more degrading. I planned my flowers they are nice out in front of the house. We had an outhouse here no inside pluming not like what we had left. We carried water from a spring in a town their dad would go to this town where everyone say is an all-black town.

I would go to the water hole to get water for the house and he would accuse me yet again for meeting and having affairs with other men. Lee was out some where drinking with his butte and wasn't home helping out when he could have went and got the water, that way he wouldn't have to wonder who I was seeing. Now some time has passed our next baby was about due to be born this house we were living in is a dump I try fixing it up good enough to live in and raise a baby.

After having my baby, I had Lee's family over for Supper one evening and I made beans, fried photos, and biscuits. And I forgot to put shorting in them and they were hard we couldn't eat them. Beth said I could knock someone out with these and she thoughted them at the house and knock out a window.

I went to the Doctor because I was feeling sick, he said in nine months you will be better, and I said what, he replied you having a baby. So that our three children that I'm carrying I did not want to hear that so soon after Tark I would have had to go then with baby #3 in sometime in July. I was sick a lot with her I couldn't ride far without getting sick. Then my baby got sick and was taken to Children hospital he must be treading there. They were this one nurse there who took to caring for him got to know use well. The Doctors at the Hospital said he will always be sick if we as parents continue to fuse and fight around them, he went on to say it not good for any of the kids in the home. So, we went home for a while to rest then Lee went to his boyfriends to drink then came back mad, why didn't I stay up there with him.

So, when we went back up to see him he had got worse. Lee wanted to go back home then I stayed there with him, he left me there and I took care of our baby in a full day they were going to release him, and Lee was nowhere to be found, of somewhere drinking. By this time, I call his Mom and she went looking for him. She found him, but he was so drunk he couldn't come. So, we were being ready to go home the next day. He came up the next morning to get use.

We came home to a dirty house it looked like a Party happen here. I don't know how many times I felt like Just giving up on this Life. One more kid was not what I wanted. I can't take care of two and keep them feed or get them what they needed. Yes, we got a welfare check. Food Stamps to help by the time drinks, smokes, and gas to run around came out there was no money left. Yes, I paid the Rent, Electric and the Phone bills.

What Lee had in the back of his mine was how many of the Doctors did I had sex with while I was there. But he didn't say anything. Cause his mother was at the house waiting for me to help me with the kids, she kept Sam while I was caring for our baby.

Now we are moving again and this time on in a nice house back in a field, and winter was coming on we couldn't get out a lot of the times, so I miss lot of my appointments. There I was going out to the outhouse and fill on a rock coming back, and I hurt myself, I didn't say anything about hurting, but I know I should have because I was worried that I hurt the baby, that Lee didn't want it was very clear he wanted nothing to do with Her my kids all of them was his.

Now it time for another baby #3 She was due in two weeks the week Turk was in the hospital he was coming home about the time I was going to have her so of to the hospital for me she came right on time March I had her faster than the 1st two doctor I had for her of greenfield was my doctor then and yet again I was having affair with him to is what I was told by Lee.

But the doctor told me something though who accuse you of being with anther is the one doing it their self. So, let give him something to worry about I want to see you every week for a checkup. You have a back problem, so I want you to sleep on your side.

Later She was born Lee didn't like her much, why I didn't know he would hit her for crying he called her bug another man names he steps in her food. When we would go down to the Mom's place she would set them all down in the floor and give them all a plate of Chips to eat, he would always step in her plate he didn't do the boy's that way. His mom saw this and got mad that what he did to her food and did not like it. She asks him why you do that to her he said I don't like her, I didn't know why until he called her bug. He was an old friend I know in school.

But I hadn't seen him in a long time. I know is sister, we were good friend and I haven't seen her.

Now we are moving to another place one no better than the last one we moved form he thought being on welfare he would have more money to spend the rented places got cheaper put the size of our family didn't it got bigger. And the rent payments got cheaper put the houses got worse not live able put his drinking got bad to I now thinking he's a real hard drinker.

The house was a bit bigger to live in lot more room for the kids we have I had the baby bed in our room so, she be close to me, the water here was full of worms I had to strain our water before we could use it we carried the water we drink and cooked with. He was so accusatory, and I wasn't happy in our life together anymore. So, to have one more baby with him wasn't what I didn't want, but I was having one more baby. I wasn't going to abort this one put I did say this one the last one.

We were over to Lee Sister the one who didn't like me, she had just got a new living room set, the plastic was still on it, and I was having labor pains, so we started for home and across the bridge and my water broke we was going to take the other kids to his Mom's, put there was no time for that. A nurse watches the other kids while I was having our baby at the hospital, I had her fast and the doctor had no time to get his gown or glove on he got there in time to catch her, the best petty baby yet. You can see she looks like you there no denying her. Doctor said she going to have a lot of problems with her.

I wanted to have a tubal done so I would have any more kids, put Lee didn't want me to so he accuses me of wanting this done so I could sleep around and not get pregnancy. they wanted someone take Jean to go home because it was time for her to leaves the Hospital, but no one wanted to take her, so I was going to be in the hospital for !0 days Doctor said keep her here in my room and she can care for her. I had to have blood and my type (HRN) was rare and putting it in me it was cold Lou stayed there with me and Lee was nowhere to be found the other kids was at grandma's. So, after the Surgery Lou came in and helped with caring for Jean When it was time for me to go home he was late getting me said the Car wouldn't start. All it need was gas, that he ran out running.

He came got me I was hurting form the surgery Put he didn't care. He wanted sex, put I refused him. I Said no. I attended with the kids needs and got Supper for all us. I told him doctor said no sex, and I'm not going to. At its time I'm 23 ages and want no more kids he said you can have sex with anyone now HNN, my reply was you said I was doing that before I got fixed, so what's changed now. After having my tubal done thing got worse more degrading.

Two weeks has pass and I wanted a Beer, so I got some now I'm drinking after all the kids now are born and here.

That night I had 3 beers and got drunk went to bed for a while. Now as he said I can horse around and not worry about having someone else kids. He won't work we are still on Welfare and food stamps.

I stayed home caring for our kids and he was out some where God know where, and here at home keeping kids happy and faded.

We have move to Breath Lane we were getting grocery at store there in the small town. I would help her in the store to help pay our bill of thing stamps wouldn't pay for Smoke, Gas, soap powders to wash with, and others. (Remember I don't SMOKE!)

I went to a restaurant to check on a Job as a Waitress, for $1.25 an Hour I liked the job and had my own money. I also like going to sales and go to yard sales to get things we needed. I waited on a lot of nice people put I was accused of wanting to have sex with them. Lee liked the money I bought home, but he didn't want me to work.

I found another Job that payed more Restaurant in Chilly as a kitchen helper and dishwasher, $2.45 an hour. My hours were 4pm to 11 pm, he was birching about the hour, but I liked my job, I worked hard to make something out of a bad home. I didn't want to be there anymore. I would to work early and come home late when I went to work early I buy my own dinner It seem I need to get away from crying kids and Birching husband.

My mother wanted me to help har clean her house, so I ask Lee to come with me, so he could watch the kids because they were always in to something. But he wouldn't come help me he wanted to go to his friends to drink. Jean was 4 she was in to things and she got hold of Mom's heart pills and took them it was hard to keep an eye on them and get any work done.

The others were outside with grandpa playing. Jean was my problem child who got hurt a lot, so we kept her in, after I was done all I could we pack up the car Sam help me with Jean, so I could drive, I went to his Mom then told her what happen, she called the squad to come get us. Ida kept the others and t told her not to let Lee come down here, he didn't care to help watch them, so t didn't want him there with us.

She didn't let him come the next day Ida broth soup and coffee for me had stayed all night with her. We were there for two night and three days the doctors wanted to make sure they had got all out of her. I left to go home for wash and put clean close on and came back. I let Ida come get us when it was time to go home. Lee was mad cause I didn't want him there. He was out we the boys my sisters drinking so I told him to keep going. Our kids meant nothing to him he wasn't there for them.

I trust Lee the kids father to watch the kids while I worked out he let one get bit by an elective cord a put it in her mouth while he was running a drill. He was working on the truck and it was raining out the kids like the rain I was at work. He wasn't paying any attention to them Turk one of the boys had to tell him something is wrong with Jean, it took a peace form her mouth. no one called me a work, no one took her to the hospital to be checked out.

I got home around 11;30 pm from work, he told me what had happen. Jean was awake, so I looked at her, put her clothes on her and took her to the hospital myself. When Jean and I got home it was around 2 am, Jean was going to be find. I contend to work for a full more weeks. There was a full more thing we still needed, three week I quit my job. By this time, I've had two jobs'. Lee had yet again accused me of not taking care of the kids, when that all I do.

I have done everything I can do, keeping kids in school shoe clothes. They didn't get new things. They got what I could afford. So, I told him, "Fine yourself a job". I'll stay home I want to any way I'll make do some sewing and make things. I'll be here when the kids get home from school. Lee said no I can't work, I said why not there nothing wrong with you. He said my back and head hurts.

I went on to say if I had a head like that I'd call the doctor. Lee went to the doctors to compline about what was hurting him, doctors couldn't find anything wrong. He just wants to stay on welfare and not work. I said we are not going to have anything, I'm tired of living in run down dump you call a house we can't heat them and hand me down furniture I want something new.

New pair of Shoes would be nice or a new dress that I couldn't afford while I was working. It took all I made and getting welfare to put clothes shoes for the kid

Now we are moving again to Lyndon in a three room house another small house. Place wasn't big enough for use Put I made it work the rent was $50. Month We took it cause the rent was cheap. Our babies were growing up we lived here for a year, Lee had put in for is benefits. Then one night he was playing with the kids doing a homogeneous with then and twitted his angle, we didn't have a running car at the time Then I went back to the lady who lived behind use to get her car and take Lee to the Hospital. She stayed with the kids she was a black woman very nice to I liked her.

She come to our house to see how we all was, and we were ok. Lee bother meth and teddy came to our place and brought this woman named Shafter ruby they all were drinking was in our bed having sex her and broke our bed down Lee know this he was watching them. Put he was accuse again saying I want teddy, meth, put I wasn't the one wanting them.

Lee benefits came thought for him we got two new or used cars, one for me a Chevy and a Ford pickup for him. Out of his check was a car and pickup. He got a lot of new thing for the kids and the house, life got a little better until the money ran out.

We found a nice house on Minnie Hill as my little girl got older they start to develop in to young ladies, so I kept my eyes on them watching them. the boys have already gown up, my girls were 6 and 7 age, so t got the boys trying thing with them. There was this basement door outside of the bedroom window, I was looking out to see what they were doing.

Piwe and tuck had the girls put their hands upon the door then the boys pulled down their pansy. I went and got a swish went outside got the girls and beat the them, then put them in the house the boys took off running put I got them and beat them to. I was upset that I had beat them I was going to call the cobs on myself. When I dial the number on the other end was my mother in law, I had told her What I did. She came over and took care of the kids and I went to the woods, took a walk. Ida stayed and got supper for the kids Lee was out running around somewhere. I felled bad after I witted the kids.

Lee got me a new washer and dryer set. But we had to sale them. He needed the money to buy a car.

We are moving yet again put this time up the road form where we are at. Windy Ridge, Rd.

Living here I was going to Church and teaching Bible study class. there I was accuse of running all the man there to. I was going every Sunday and till I quit going then some of the women folk came to the house to see if I was ok. We set there and talked for some time, the people at the Church knower my problems about Lee and how he accuses me.

There was this one night going to Church out of my drive my dog was following me, and I didn't know it. It was raining outside, I hit her, she was due for Baby's I stopped had a nice white dress on I picked her up and carried her back to the house put her in her bed, I went back to my car and Went on to Church that night, wet dirty form the mad, and feeling bad, everyone in that Church looked at me then the preachers wife came to me and ask what happened. I told then what had happened Then everyone they Prayed for me and my dog that night.

The next 3 days my dog was up and moving about, I took that as a good sign she going to be ok. 3 weeks she had her puppy, she had 6 babies'. I had no trouble giving the pup's away. People at the Church wanted them. So that this time I know the **Power of Parys Works**.

By this time, I know how to work and care for MY kids, by myself. The kids are now going to school and I could work while there in school. I went out to find a job where I could work while kids were in school. The hours had to be 7am to 3pm. he didn't work so I wanted him to watch them for a full hour until I got home. But he didn't want to.

So, I ask around to see if he was old enough to stay with them for a full hour after school. He watches them it was ok. If I thought, he was able. Some and I set down to explain the job to him and his pay. Him for the 1st time did a good job. I was very proud of him.

Lee saw a house he wanted us to buy and they wanted $$ Down like a land contract deal. We ware to pay $300 month buying the place. I did a lot of think in on this but Lee on Social security disabled, so I said want you lose your money, so he said no I'm aloud to make soon. so now he got a job at Lumber Co. to make the money we needed for the down payment. I saw selling Rubber Maid produces I had to go around for parties, I really enjoyed this job cause I got to see other people and sell. Lee went with me to some of the parties, why he didn't trust me to be with women.

Down the road always lived my sister and Lee brother Jay, they didn't have water there at their place, so they came to our house to get water or Jay did a lot. He would come up while Lee went to work, and the kids was in school. And take advantage of me. Lots of times I wouldn't let him in. this happen ed a lot time he come get water. I didn't tell Lee because he would had said it was my flout anyway and I didn't want to put a damper on their friendship.

I had a car I wanted to remodel so Lee said get Jay to help you with it and I thought to myself that not what I wanted I was hoping Lee would help with it. Lee had already talk to Jay to help me with the Car. Yes, he more than happy to help me with is car. I was always affair to be left alone with him when he came get water. This was every morning.

It was an old 1969 Dodge Charger car, after the kids went to school he would come unto help me with the car, leaving her at the house. So, we begin taking prats of to see what we needed to go get for it, me in my short shorts and small tops under a car was a piling to him taking out the transmission to replace it. We went to the junk yard to get some parts needed for this car lots of times.

I thought Lee trusteed Jay because he was here all the time, he didn't say anything about him for being here helping with the car and getting water. But later I found out I was Wrong, Lee did accuse me of having Jay sexily. Thing and my feeling started to change for Lee. I did get closed to Jay put not as a lover put a good friend. Jay saw always around when I needed something done.

Jay and I did become very good friends as we were working together on the car. I had fun working with him on this Car.

I got an anther job to help raise money, but we didn't all the money we needed for the down payment of the house. I went to town an took out a loan for the down payment. I couldn't believe that I could get the money. But I did, get a loan I took 2 jobs in restaurants day and night to help get it money. Lee was still on his SSI check currently and working. Because the social security disability dept, said you could make so much extra money, he worked. So, we got the house, payments were $316. a month and the loan were $240 month. Ins, $15. Month by this time our bills had Double up.

Well we move into this house and all the water pipes needed fixing right away. The former owner did help fix the pipes, he didn't want to. but we couldn't afford to have them fixed was the former owners of this place. I love the house, but I didn't get to spend much time there, for I was always working. It was up to me to make all the payments, so we wouldn't lose the house.

Lee Quit his job as a lumber co. because they couldn't get Insurance on him. So, he said. They told him he was an accident waiting to happen so now he can't help with any of the bills. He still has his check for how long we don't know cause the social security disability dept has contacted him.

Now that I was working three jobs I needed someone to watch the kids cause their father was not relivable to care for them. So, I was looking for a baby sitter to stay with them and found a couple who wanted the job. We take to them or I did. And they didn't drink speech foul language in all they were what I wanted two of the nicest kids to watch my kids. I was at ese knowing they was there with them.

I got this couple to work, when I would pay them for working they wanted to take the kids out for a treat like Ice-cream or to the play grounds to play. These baby sitters were good for my kids seen I couldn't be home and was always working somewhere. Every time I paid these kids they took my kids out for pop and chips and have a small party of it. The kids love them, so I had then over for dinner a lot when I could.

The lade owner came up when the leaves were fulling and we hadn't had time to clean up the yard, yet we were both busy trying to keep up with the payments for this place. I was getting very tired; my mom had died in February of 81. My grandma had gone in 79. thing was starting to get to me. Lee got fried from his job with the trailer place. I'm still working two jobs trying to keep thing going. Lee would not find another job all the Bills was due, Electric $255. I couldn't pay it. We were behind on our house, loan payment everything else was coming dues I was tried and upset I didn't know what else to do. Come October lady owner was birching about the yard and she went to the Social Security Dept. And cause Lee to lose his check. I feel that she wanted us to lose this place. I said this will hurt you far more than it wills us. Now Lee has no income do to working And Jan help.

Now it November our electric is off for a bill of $275. house and loan payment is behind a full month, but the insurance is payed up for a full month. The only thing I know to do is hang it up and guilt my jobs because I can't do it by myself. I didn't think buying a home would be this bad or hard to do.

So, the moral of this story doesn't try something like buying a home with no money coming in. If you need to work 3 to 4 jobs to pay for it not worth it.

Now it coming to December still no electric, we have heat with a wood stove and I cooked on the wood stove. Christmas was approaching, but I could not get any help anywhere. Some one finds out our hard ship and sent help. We got buckets of food clothes toys, came pouring in from everywhere. we set up a tree that year without lights, that Christmas eve my dad and brother Ron came up to the house seen there was no light on the tree, so dad ask wares your light I said no electric, at that time dad said I'll be back. When a full hour went by and dad with a whole lot of people came with him.

I could not believe what I was seeing. More lights for the tree lantanas candles, food clothes toys came in again we got a lot of help. Then this one man said if you can get by without electric 5 more days I'll get this back on for you. My reply was yes Thank you. We were not without light for the rest of that year.

For that Christmas we went to Lee Mom's for Dinner took a full of the thing we got there to fix for the dinner, we got 3 turkeys, pies and cake mixes. It was five more days to January and we planned on going there for help.

We were on welfare before. I went to see if we could get some help with our electric bill. She Said we can help you, but it would cost $105. For recanted your electric. Can you wait tell after Christmas break? I said we been out without three months 5 more days.

The day we went back on welfare and food stamps we went looking for something to rent we move 3 times before finding a nice place. One was beside a horse mam who he helps for little extra cash the house was a total dump. Hard to heat. No water. So, we went out looking again for a home and find this one on lower twin rd. nice big farm looking place I liked it one had a bath room running watering in the house, it was close to the road and kids was small.

The man who owned it lived in Bainbridge, the rent was $135. Month, this man came to see us and said if you still want the house it's yours, so we paid the rent that day. Coming March, we Started to move in there 3 bedrooms upstairs nice big eat in kitchen all the rooms were roomy. We live there the longest of any place else.

We met a lot of people here, we were back on welfare and food stamps and got a medical card for the kids. $425. Check so we could pay our rent and electric bills these was the only two bills we had. The house was big Three room up and 4rooms bath down. Big yard barn, an outhouse. We got some horses, we had two before we moved here. Life here went on as normal. I wanted to take the girls to the doctor to find out why the was still wetting the bed, at their age 9.10 I was worried. A friend told me of this doctor who treats bedwetters, in greenfield who could help them. So, I took them to see her.

Here's where a lot of trouble started for our home, after taking the girls to this doctor, she said the girls had a disease's that can only be got by sexual She was 10 and when the doctor checked her, I went in the room with the girls. The doctor told this I did not know what to say or do at that time. Well the doctor asks Her how you got this, she didn't know what to say or what the doctor was talking about she just a kid I didn't know what the doctor was talking about either, so I ask her what diseases this is. Leases infesting at you get form man playing with you. She was so frightened and was wanting her dad. She said Daddy did this then the doctor took that her dad did it. At this time the doctor office called the welfare child service to come out to our home. The doctor did say went the girls are touch like this they will continue to wet the bed.

My Blood pressure went out the roof at day so someone from the child services was at the house before I got home with the kids, they look all over the house then talk to us all. After seeing where the girls sleep with us in the 1st. bedroom.

Lee had to leave the house move out, so he packed a full thing and waited for the boys to come home from school.

Then he went to his sister Beth to stay there for a full week. The Boys didn't know why their daddy was leaving nor did they know what happen that day. I took the boys up to their Ann Saturday to visit with their dad. When I could I set them all down to expend thing to them, best I could. I felt they were all mad at Her, I think I was to, But I knower deep in my heart it couldn't be true.

Now a full week went by and everyone was hurting about their dad leaving the house. I call out Family doctor to get a 2nd appendant He sent all 6 of us to the get lab work and a complete piss test. Jones didn't find any sexily disease, just a yeast infection. But the children service still wouldn't let Lee come home while She was still in the home, now in our Three weeks apart.

Lou and I got to talking about this and she said let Her come stay here with me till we can get thing straighten out. So, I pack up some things for her thing and when she got home from school I told the kids what we were going to do. She is going to Lou's to live for a while till we can get thing back where the belong. so we all whet to Lou took Her in there I felt like I was abending her but to keep all the kids happy I know not else to do. Then your daddy can come back here with the rest of you.

I got the feeling Lee wanted to go to Jail for something he thought he did. For what I didn't know I don't think he know either. But I couldn't fix his problem, Hell I couldn't fix mine I had a quit a full of them. She wanted people to quit arguing and messing with her mine about her. At the time we all had this break up She had a boyfriend she was seeing down the road them. But I didn't think she was done anything with him. She had started her Lady hood in February. She acted like a girl who had already had sex with who. I didn't know. I started a new job with a nursing home in Frankfort, as an aid caring for people I worked night form 11pm to 7am. While Lee their daddy could take care of the kids all he had to do was get was be there I put then to bed before I went to work. Then get them up for school and get his self of to work. He worked under the table, so he could make all the money he wanted, and he use it to. For dirt bike dune buggies, and any other toy he wanted. I got off at 7am and was home by 8am. I worked for 3 months and then got laid off.

So, we went back on welfare until I wanted to go back to school and get my GED. So, I could get a better job. I went out to the career& technology school. I saw an ad in the paper for the business collage to get a GED. I whet there to check it out I wanted to sign up for these class. I talked to Lou about this because I could talk to her about what I wanted.

I could never talk to Lee about anything because he wouldn't listen to me. Lou wanted to go to, so we went together that was ok if Lou went to. We sign up for 3 qt. and started on our GED My first qt. was 3 months. I took the GED class 1st. My last month it was test time.

I was studying day and night to get it all in my head. I went over to Lou's a lot we would study together. I tested on Saturday and got a 191 adage I need a 200 to pass. I continue to study cause I needed to get this for me. There other class here in this school I wanted but I need by GED. 1986

I was setting down stairs one night as I do most of my night because I can sleep some night went something on my mine. So, this one night I was studying had all my books out on the couch I had been working for some time the kids and Lee was all in bed. I got up and got me something to drink I got me some milk then went back and set down got my books started to work. I was setting on the sofa studying for about two hours.

Lee and the kids were upstairs asleep. I heard someone walking upstairs I thought someone was coming down to the bathroom. So, I set there for a while, but no one came the walking stopped. I said well maybe they went back to bed. so, they change their mine. I went to get me some more milk then went back in and sat down on the sofa.

I heard the walking again. I suspected the boys because I always cote then in their room. I sat my milk down and my books and went upstairs to see what was going on, I kept a wooden bat under my bed for this reason To Protect my girls. Went in to the girl's room and as I pulled back the bat back and ready to hit then but I stop and thought what that would do to me and going to Jail was not one of them there was the light switch, something told me turn it on. I did you would not believe what I saw, standing over Lynn no panty cover on her and Lee with no clothes on and on top of her. I have two girls in this bed and the boys in the room next to them.

After I cote him I made him get down stair. He said he was just checking on them that not what I saw. I couldn't sleep for days after that it was so upsetting to me. So, the next day I ask him to leave the house I was very pissed. I had heard of fathers who have sex with their own kids. I had wonder how long this was going on while I was at work. After he went down stairs I dress her with her sleepers that she was wearing when I put them to bed. So, I check on both girls Jean still had her thing on, Then I covered them. went down stairs act him Why, **Why.**

Lee had nothing to say for his self. I didn't speak to him for I was mad and about to cry.

After I got myself together I ask him WHY again Lynn is 14 at this time and jean 13 Both petty little lady's Lee excuse was I was sleep walking.

But I didn't want to believe He would do that to our kids, I had trusted him to watch them while I worked, and when they were all asleep.

I don't believe that for a moment What would you have done if I would had hit you with the bat. Lee said you should have, why did you do something I didn't know about. I said if I had you would have died, and I would have gone to jail. Then the kids would have no one. Do you know how that makes me feel you wanting your own girls for sex?

How many other times have you done this, I worked night, and this made me look like a very bad mom. I couldn't sleep at nights thing of what happen with the kids I realty could tell if he felled bad of what I saw with my eyes. He didn't want this in me. The more I tried to forget what happen and more hurt I felled. I didn't tell anyone of what happen that night, there was no one I could trust with my life about what was bothering me.

There was one person who cared about me and my feeling, so I went to her. She saw I was upset and that something was wrong, I told her what had happen that night with Lee and the girls after talking with her a lot was lifting form my heart she had no answer for me put she listen to and heard what I had to say I feel a little better after getting it out. How many times had he done this while I was at work. Only god knows, and he wasn't going to tell me.

The moral of it story is don't trust your man of the house dad or others to be watching you girls or boys. I will tell you what I find out about the boys later in this story.

Now Lou and I continue our schooling for the GED classes but after the 3 qt. we quit, our loans run out form the Grant we got. We went to the bank to get a student loan. But we spent it for everything but school. Funny no I'm not going back to school said Lee I didn't finch my classes.

Now here how I felled no work, no love, no help, and can't trust my husband to help with anything. **I'm a FAILER!** I can't do anything or see anything good happing for me here. At this time of my life I feel like just giving it all up, but my best friend Lou wouldn't let me.

I change the job to day work form 7am to 3pm so I could be home at nights and watch my kids, I no longer want him stay with the kids someone who use then for sex toys don't need kids. I was there when they got on the bus and when home they got home. I did the house work like washing closes and getting dinner all the other thing that needed doing. Lee was no good with doing any of the house work. I had said I'm going to leave and take the kids you don't care about them anyway. I wasn't working any more for all he wanted to do was accuse me of wanting every man out there.

I packed up the car and went to my mom's place took the kids to. But he came over to moms and said you can't do this come home. I went back home where didn't want to be. I really had no other choose in this matter, I couldn't raise these kids be myself. I could not get the pass out of my head of what he had done to the kids. I Felled so Lost. The love I ones felt for him was all gone he had hurt me so much in the pass with all the accusing, the kids, no matter what I did nothing was right. I would go somewhere I was accused of having sex with whoever was there.

I got hostile and grumbly I was always mad. I didn't want anything to do with him. With my school money he wanted me to buy him a garbage route. My bother wanted to sale the route, so Lee would have a job. I bought the route and he did work it. My brother was thinking of me when he wants to sale, so he could go work and I would stay home. By this time, I leant a new way to make some extra money.

Wild root hunting so I got a sack and fork went to the woods to gather red root. I just wanted to see how far away from house I could get. I didn't know Why, I just did. Lee made some money on the route and spent it for beer before he got home. The route went good for a while and after that I went with him to get the money, so it wouldn't be wasted we made a lot thought days. Then the it was summer time we let the boys go help him on the route. Then the girls and I went to the woods to gather roots red roots was $2.50 a pound at this time.

The boys were helping their dad with the route and know where people kept their money for the payment. Then the boys stated to still the money form the route, Lee said people wasn't paying their bills. So, I started to go back on the route with him and found out that the kids with their friends was coming to get the money. So, at this time we needed to sell the route cause with kid taking the money we had nothing to run it with. We got $500. For it.

I want to start a business of my own, but I couldn't afford it. Lee said, you can't run a business anyway. Little did he know. I said," Find." I gave up on that ideal cause he puts everything down I want to do. Like I'm not good enough to do.

We are still living in this nice House. And down the road form use moves in a couple who had lots of kids. they started to come meet use for we had no friends here to talk to. Their names were Lar and Can, they became betty good friends, can had a baby she breasts feed and all Lee could do was stare at her tits Lee and the boys sat and watched her feed the baby all the time. Turk and pewee would go to her house, so they could watch her tits come out Something new to do woopy. Can would come to our house all the time and told use what Tuck had said look at thought big blue vines in your tits. there would come up to play a game of Aggressive ion, this is one we all played before our neighbors, came to join us. The kids loved playing this one some would get mad cause they lost but we went on playing.

We had both found good friends with Lar and Can someone we could talk to. On the day our car broke down we had no other we of going after parts for our car. That the time we owned a blue dodge charger we had over hull the engine. We need more part to get it running, and it was going to rain out. Lar had a motorcycle was is only way getting around. So, Lee didn't want to ride with him to go get the part. it started to rain, and Laree had a rain cape, we stopped at his home to get it. I put my arms around him and he covered us.

So, I went with Lar to Chillicothe to get what we needed. Lar has high blood pressure and take med. For this. I said to Lar if you didn't take a lot of med. You be a lot of fun. This got back to Lee and he took it the wrong way. Yet again accusing me of wanting Lar. Lar like me any way, but as a friend I know this I like him too.

But when we got back with the parts for the car, it. We didn't get back still late cause we had to stop for the rain, but it was late when we got started. Lee said why did you stop by the trailer, I told him to get the rain cape, I didn't go in Lar went in for the rain gears we wouldn't get wet. He didn't believe me no surprise.

Can. stayed at the house with Lee and the kids, So I said What did you do while I was gone, he said nothing, but the kids' faces told a different tale. Now that we are back they started to work on the car the next day. Fixing this car took 3 days to do. But now it back together. Thank God.

I ask Lee why to do you accuse me of wanting everyone I encounter. Can and Lar had been good friends to us.

well they came nervy day all day and stay. We had no time for mush else

One day our friends were moving out going to town to live, we didn't see them any more after that. We didn't keep any friends because Lee was always wanting to hit then for looking at me. Our lives were back to where it was Borings as hell. We had lived here on lower twin for 6 years is the longest time we stayed anywhere. And being on welfare our income was limited to what we could have.

I started treatments at the crises center I needed someone to talk to about thing, like the kids and why their father did these things to kids. My one question was why you would fine soap in little boy's beds. The answer I got men us this to play with their kid's dick I was so out of it.

Now yet again we moved again just above the levy Road in the old house I grow up in. This one was where Mom died in 1981. of food poising. I had been taking care of Mom and giving her Shots she needed, then one day Sis was going to her treatments in Columbus,

Then Mom wanted to spend the day with her Sister who lived in Chilly, so she took her there. Mom didn't drink Milk with her food she drinks Beer, and after being there for the day. Sis stopped and got Mom Bought her home and Mom wasn't feeling good as my dad said. Three days after Mom's outing with her Sister She died, in 81 and if I had known that milk would have saved her I would pored a gallon down her. But I did not know this until she was going. We found out she eat food at her Sisters that was Bad.

We moved again This place had no running water in the house, we moved from one that had everything we needed for a house cause the rent went up to $150. A month, he wanted something cheaper. We could pay the rent and all the other bills put that left no extra cash for him to piss away. Or (Drink up.)

The rent for the old home stead was $50. Month. There was and outside toilet to use, and for water we carried in form a well of upper twin rd. This place did have a fell thing like a chicken house and big garden for planting. Everyone wanted to help with the garden put when it came time to do it no one wanted to help. I prayed to have it ready for planting, so I did all myself. Pulling feeds form the garden was the herded job so while it was raining and got thing wet I'd go out without shoes on in my bear feet and pull weeds the kids help me they thought it was fun playing in the rain. Well we did get the weeds out and had a good garden after that. Thank you, Kids, for your help.

I wanted to Open and a Game room where kids could go and get off the streets to play pool. I did open one rented a building of Benner and opened. I open the Hall and on my grand opening night A big winder storm came in and I had all the Kids that night. People was coming from everywhere, to the game room it was the safest place to be.

This was April my opening night, I took in more money that night. The cops everywhere were Closing all the bars and shops in Bainbridge. There look in my place and seen I had all the kids that night and divided to leave me open. Lee was helping all the Cops to get then home and off the streets the roads was getting very bad that night.

There was around 12 Sheriffs in this town working to get people home and off the streets. My place was packed with big and little people till 2;45. That morning. They kept me open for the kids. As I had all the kids that night I was making money my own kids help me that night was surprising all pool game was .25 cent and we had to rack then for who was playing the game there was 6 tables to watch.

People was running around trying to get people home, Lee went to get Beth and kids to take them home. I was enjoying my new job, but this hurts Lee because I found something that for fills me and make me happy.

Lee started is Bitching, Arguing and accusing me of running men and boys at the pool hall, it seems I can win with him. My thought on this is he going out with other women and having affairs so he thing I do it.

The moral of this story is if he is accusing you then he's doing it himself. So, take a good look at how he acks.

I did keep the Pool hall open for years working it was the most fun I had had. Sept. I closed the pool hall.

With the money I saved form the pool hall I wanted an anther business, so I went out hunting for another building to rent for a Shop. I found one 2 rooms and bath, for $80. Month rents. I rented it and people from all over help me get tables and thing to set it up. I know the Festival was coming to town the next month of October, so I want to have thing ready for it and I did. I was doing consignments for people, so everyone bought things in. for me to sale for then I had help that week in form the town people. All went well good week end.

Thank you for the shop I opened.

After I quit the pool hull something happens Labor Day week end She want to go stay the week end with her cousin who live in small town. I was not an easy with it, cause a bar right there in front of their home and Lynn was Hot to trot any way, I feared the worse would happen and It did. She went to the bar a got with the wrong people and was taken away form use.

No one had seen or heard from her in weeks. We went everywhere looking for her put could not find her. Her friend in which she was to stay didn't know where she had gone. She was lost to us for some time now and opening the shop was getting hard. But I had to. The School made up Flyers to put out to find her.

Our first thought that was that she run away, or that someone had killed her. We didn't know what had happened. Thoughts of losing a child was hurting to mothers, we carry them protect then form harm and then someone take them away. I worried about my baby for six weeks and while the Festival someone saw the Flyer in this big town and know she was our lost baby. Large was on his way to get her. Thank You God for being her home.

Want to Thank the Town of Bainbridge & School for the flyers for your help in finding my baby. The moral of this story Trust your gut if one of you want to stay with a friend.

I had made that one-week end $500. Which went out to fine Her. How they find her is a bar man there ask her how she got this far from home, the bar keep seen her picture on tv missing report, she went to us the rest room and he locked her in there and called Chillicothe. Large went and got her took her to judicial hall till court was set. We weren't allowed to see her yet, but she was home. We all went to the court room Monday for her and they want to know why she did this, but she couldn't tell them anything because she was afraid to say anything. Well she back home and back in school. She had been using drugs up there she was taken to the hospital for a checkup and Tasted for everything.

She told us she got in a car of guys with a bottle of Mad dog liquor and they took her to somewhere she didn't know. They would not bring her back down here after all Her problems was behind her, I tried again to leave home.

I had packed my thing and Had them in the car I went to Lou's place but again Lee follow me there he couldn't stand the fact that me and Lou was the best of friends.

Now again I'm where I don't want to be so sick and tired of the bitching arguing and accusing form this thing who says he a man bull shit. Tared of all the Man of it house Running around getting drunk, with other women and accusing me when I'm the one with the kids.

These kids with me at the shop most of the time Otherwise, they were at the house where Lee was caring for them while I worked. I was told that I couldn't take care of my kids. If I hadn't done some of the things I did, we would not have made it. This kept my kids in food and a home.

Lee didn't Trust me to run my own shop, he came up and set across the street from the shop watching to see who came in and out of the place. To me this was so invariant. Later that year I got ahold of all the people I was selling for and had then come get there thing because I was choosing the shop. I gave all the clothes away I had taking in.

I sold out the rest of what I had. My shop was now closed, all because I couldn't be Trusted. Said's Lee

The moral of this story is doesn't aloud a man tell you, you can't do something show him. We women have more back bone then Men.

You see I'm not a quitter I wanted to start yet another business, there was this lady who was wanting to start a Flea Market and wanted to be part of it to. So, she had a field on the out skirts of Bainbridge I met with a Friend on the east of town for the market. We waited until after the sale of the Big Building and bought the small ones building she had pulled onto her place. Then she got eight more small building and I was to care for them and rent them out, I got a building to sale form to.

By April we were open the building rented for $45. month. and I had them all rented and others setting up on the grounds. I had to set up a full thing to sale before I could get a building.

My set up was $3. A day outside, a full other people set up to outside. There was two nice guys men, had ask me if I wanted to run a building for them and I could put my things in there to. and get a % of what I sold for then 20 to 25% was what I would make. I didn't see anything wrong with this ideal selling for them. I was making more money and enjoyed what I was doing. They went to actions houses to get thing and bring them back to me at the flea market where I was working for them. The two with whom I worked for. They put up shelfs in the building and fix it up for a sale barn.

So, we got all our things in there when open I would set something out side. I did all the Pricing, selling because they both worked other job and didn't have time. They know me form picking up cans on the roads, and we got our dog feed and thing for our horses at his store.

Lee 's over possessiveness', jealousy, is hard to take at times. he started his shit all over again accusing and arguing, why, because I was working for two men who was hardly there, they trusted me with their money and thing I sold for them. Put Lee couldn't have trusted me with them, they come by on Sunday evening to get their money and pay me for selling. That was the only time I saw them.

My 4 kids are all grown up now and out of school so that leaves us without an income. I got out and walk the roads pick up cans and dig wild roots to help buy smokes and gas for man toys, mine you I don't smoke or drink. Now why did I get out and go can hunting? To get away from the house of a mouthy man. I wanted so badly to get lost, lost never to be found.

My oldest girl was with a baby, due in 1/91, she was still living at home and I was still working the Flea Market in Bainbridge I was still taking a lot of the mouthing me, but I leant to cope with it. Well month went by fast and Lynn had her baby a new year Boy, then Lee wanted me to quit my job and raise a kid he tries to take over the baby as if it was his baby, he wouldn't let her take him anywhere. I'm still working the flea market and I didn't want to raise someone else kids. It Her baby let her raise him, she moves out of the house and took him with her. She couldn't take any more of the shit either.

Then Lee would go get him and bring him back here, so I said if you want him you raise him. He said I don't trust her to take care of him. what it boiled down to and I have always said he don't trust anyone with his kids yes, I said His. Yet today that how I feel. I did trust her cause he was her 1st. baby and she needed to learn how to care for her kids. I didn't want to raise him, so she could go out Drink and Drug run around.

We were living on Scott Road currently.

How I ended up with him and his money, back on welfare and raising her baby was not my Ideal. Lee wanted him, so he should take care of him. I'm still doing Flea marketing went out to action places despite hell. I just was not going to set under her baby and Lee. My 2nd. Year of work come October the Festival of leaves was coming town. I had planned to do a cook out and had 4 building to care for. Lot of work needed done so the kids came to help me with the cook out.

The two men was there that day to help me get thing ready. They stayed to help set thing up in all out barns, so we all made money. Then broth a lot of things to sale in their barn. There were mowers and people taping of the grounds for people to set up and sale. Thing was coming together good. I set my cook out in between me and the men building, so we could both watch it.

Cause the two men was helping me get thing set up Lee came up and was mad, piss because they were there. I ask Lee why you like this you could have come and help me get thing ready put you didn't want to. The men saw him come in but stayed back because they know how he is went it come to me and other men. Lee got mad, he said you need to pick them or me, I said what are you saying so I pick my job.

I did not care what he thought of me anymore I was sick of he's bulls. After he left the men ask if I was ok, they watch that he was not going to hit me. They ask you Alright I said yes, I'm fine But I wasn't. one of them know I wasn't ok, He know of the abuse I go thought and put up with form him. He went on to say if you need help or someone to talk to you know where I'm at. He won't hit you where I'm at.

I went back to working on the day of the Festival, all my kids were there to help me. It was a good week end we took in $300. That was my money. This was the last year of the flea market, I felt Lee was taking everything from me. I was Lost without my active, I saw one of the men everywhere I went, he spooks to me when he seen me. Lee got or was so very Jealous of the two men I worked with. Now by this I felled my life is over.

My last year of the flea marketing Lee got mad cause I went to the action with a women friend. He said we was just running around me and her got to be good friends and she went to the bingo halls a lot. She asks me if I had ever been to bingo before, and I said no. I just wanted out of that house I hated to be home. Going to bingo with her was a good Ideal for me to get out. She come pick me up on her way we go to bingo. I had no money, so she paid for my cared and shared the money, when I win I give her the money and then she gives it back to me.

I didn't want to take it because I wasn't going to get to use it. No sooner I got home he act you win any money. I thought I would say no put I didn't. I give him $10. Dollars of it and said that all I got. He asks why she played for the cares I played. It was her money not mine.

Back in 91, when Lee wouldn't let our daughter care for her baby, I felt he was using it as an excuse to keep me in the house. Plan my getaway, booth a small trailer, For $100. It needed a lot of work. there was no room for the baby, so she had to look for a place to take her baby. This was the only way she was going to get to keep the baby.

I had thing pack up I wanted to keep in boxes setting in a corner of the house later I got a good job. caring for the elderly lady's, form 9am to 12 noon. Pay was $63. Week which was plainly for me. I rented a Storage room without him knowing about it, I'd take a full box and put them in the car than take to the room Locked it. I had the room for 3 months before he knows the corner was getting smaller I had taken 1 to 2 boxes at a time of my things each time I went to work. I took thing I would need for 1 sleeping room. I know I had to get the thing out of the house if I wanted to keep then, he was selling everything to buy smokes and drinks.

I also had a list of phone numbers of rooms for rent and a list of places I could get help. I took a 2nd job to get extra money to pay rent on the room I was looking for one only have one bill. Lee saw the corner was clearing out and ask me what was going on with the thing. So, I told him I rented a storage room to put thing in, I know we could not take the thing to the small trailer. We didn't have room for these things then I said to him these was a flea market thing and I'm going to go setting up and sale these things. He tries to make me out of a layer. Said the key's I had was for someone s house.

I said they are not and I can prove it so one day he wanted to put some of his thing in storage before we moved to the small trailer of a dump, he tried to say this is a room I was meeting and sleeping with someone in. so we went down, and I got my keys, one for the gate, and one for the room so he saw. this pissed him off, and I was mad myself of him thinking how he felled. After this I kept taking thing to the storage room and putting thing away. I thought to myself I'm going to have all my thing

To starting my new life, seem we had to move anywhere we could not take everything. I was working 2 jobs currently putting money back for my getaway when I go to work I'd fine myself not wanting to go home. I was always saying I wish I didn't have to go home, I hated my home. By this time, I was a very unhappy person, I didn't like myself at all. Felt like a frailer at life. I just wanted to end my life one day I got Lee gun and was going to use it. I was always sick weak, but I couldn't quit. I still had thing to do and kids to care for. Lee to care for to. One Saturday night my women friend came by and wanted to go to the action.

I had always told her I would go with her when she wanted to go. That night I went with her, it didn't matter anymore to me what Lee thought he thing I'm gay anyway, because I go out with women friends, I like the action house and because the two men I liked was there which made it more enjoyable. We went a full Friday and Saturday nights.

The moral of this story Don't let some men get you so down you want to kill yourself. Just leave get out. There'll get over it.

Lynn called and wanted me to come over to look at some sweepstake paper she got in her mail. Lee know I was going to the action with my women friend that night, so he got mad, because I didn't go with him. When I got home he didn't go anywhere and stayed up.

I went to bed and on Sunday morning when I got up, I hadn't had my 1st cup coffee yet Lee said you changing aren't you. I ask him what you mean, he said what I said you are changing. I didn't say anything more I let it be all day. I know what he was trying to say I'm a Lesbian. We went to his moms for that Sunday dinner and when we got back home. Turk was there and so I ask Lee what you meant, when you said I'm changing, he didn't answer me. So, I said," What did you call me? a lazy bitch?" he said however you take it. I was hurt very bad.

I only have two female friends and he jealous of both of then his sister and new friend. She went to her home in Florida, I wanted to go with her cause she was coming right back she was checking on her husband who cat live up here with her. I just wanted to get away for a full day, she left around Thanks giving I didn't see her for a while. Now my other friend Lee don't like his sister he probity me to see her after my work I go to her home and I stay to long all we did was play cards. She was someone I could really talk to about anything. She didn't care what he thought.

I wasn't allowed to go there but I went anywhere. I feel bad sick and tired and mad, so I quit my 2nd. Job in August we didn't have the money coming in that we had.

October my birthday was coming up use to make my own cake and have the kids' home for a small party. put I just did not feel like myself, everything I liked doing was gone.

All the kids were married and out on their own living their own life's. I felled the kids didn't care anymore for me their mom, all they think of the one who hurt then dad. After all that has happened the Festal was coming to town again and I set up at the Flea market, so I set up with Two men's building My kids was there for a while. they went up town to walk around in the town. I didn't sale a lot, I couldn't talk to people like I uses to, Lee was watching my every move I made.

Thanksgiving came around I cooked. I was still hurting and needed help getting dinner put he was no help. I went to work the next week after the 25th. Of November me and the old lady I took care of got in argument. so that was my last day with her. Went I walked out the door she said I see you tomorrow. I said going out I don't think so. I know she hear me! I went to Lou's home she was going to go Christmas shopping, but she knows something was wrong.

She said you want to go get a beer somewhere. Yes, why not, we were only going to have 2 beers, but she met a friend in the bar. We got drunk that afternoon. Later we got beer to go out to the Camp Grounds, to a party. We Listen to some music. We all got drunk we could not drive home and we couldn't go to Her home, so we rented a motel room here in town, stayed there all night I slept in the chair that night.

The next morning, we went back out to the bar started drinking again. Around 3pm Sunday we did go home. We both got hell for being out Lee was mad, Lou's husband left but he came back. He wanted to know why we went drinking I was hurt so bad I had quit my job, I was always crying about something what I didn't know.

Lee was keeping a gun under his pillar and I was always afraid of it. He had this gun and I know this, so I was afraid he would find me and Lou to hurt us. I did quit my jobs. stayed with him, he kept saying you was with someone. But I put wasn't. I had played pool with the man in the bar, but I didn't sleep with then.

I don't care for sex or love form Lee any more hell he accrues Lou's for our troubles, but she is not the blame, I could tell him, but he just could not here me. to Lee it everyone else fraud not his. He drinks run around with my sisters and gets drunk.

I call the crisis intervention center for help and told then I wanted to end my life. To get out of this trap I was in I got me an appointment to see someone. I saw a consult to talk about me. On December I saw her. I went every 2 weeks to see her for me she got me up open about what was going on.

Jean got married December after that I said to myself, I'm going to do something for me. For Christmas we when to his moms for dinner. I called my brother to talk about moving in the bus, he had there. We didn't have a Phone in our home, wasn't allowed one.

Sam took a job at the park dam as care taker and I would drive him to work Then go to a friend's house after I dropped him off. I got to know him a lot more then I should have. We still had the Flea Market. we became more then Friends that year. I love it and wouldn't have change anything.

I got the small trailer for him because I know I was leaving and he would have a place to live. He had a small camper setting out side of this place and I would go to this to work on my school work, put that made him mad too. Why, I wasn't where he could see me. Then he sold that Camper and the people who got it took it to the Junk yard. I wanted to keep it looked better than the Trailer.

My brother Had a bus, said come on over it setting here. I wasn't ready yet for the move out. he kept me from doing this moving at this time. I had plan on starting my Nursing school classes I needed to get 75 hours in for class to be a nurse home health aide. I had it all planed out for my new life. I wanted this, so I could get a good job. Work and get my own place in town. I studied and pass most of my Testes.

Feb, I was studying for my test which I needed to pass. On Friday night I was so tired, and I went to bed, Lee was drunk and came in and started bothering me. I couldn't go to sleep after that. When I did go to sleep he came back in the room and woke me up. He wanted sex form me, I told him I'm tired not to night, he got mad and went out of the room. But he came back in and demanded it, you aren't going to sleep until I let you, so he Raped me that night and hurt me, **yes hurt me.**

Feb. sat, I said, and I meant it I'm moving out, I did pack what I needed and wanted to put thing in my Car. I told him I'm going to my brothers and stay in the bus. For a full week. Lee helped me packed the car, so I could leave, now the car is ready to go, and I was to. Lee wanted me to take him to Bainbridge to is sister, so I did, when he got out of the car I looked back thought my mere and saw a dog I had dump out he look like a lost puppy.

I went on over to my bother and move in the bus. A friend help pulled a load of my thing to the bus for me. Before I left he said you'll going to end up at Lou's. Lee kept coming over to my bothers wanting to talk. He told him I didn't have to talk to him and I will call the sheriff on him. He just wouldn't leave me alone.

My brother was going to town Monday I got a bag together and my books, put then in his car then I had him take me to the help Center house for help. Form there I was taken to a safe house for my safe keeping until I could get out of town. There I was given a job to do so I would have money when I got to anther safe house.

I had one more day of school for my testing. I was taking by cab to school we went thought the sheriff's office

Lee and the kids were called the school to see if I was there. They all came out there with guns day of finals to shoot up the school. Lee demanded that I come out, but the teachers put me in a room with no windows.

Then they put the rest of the school on lock down. The VA cops was called to the school where they all was told to get of the grounds. They left, and I got to finch my test with the rest of the class, after I was done and was graded I pass the test, how I was very upset. Then when it was time for me to go back to the safe house a cop come got me.

Kay pick me up there and we went back to safe house to get my thing together and she wanted to talk to me. My bother bought my car in to town for my getaway, by 4pm, I was on my way out of town the sheriff's office followed me to the country line. I continue my way to the safe house in Gallia country I was 65 miles from home.

I learn a lot about myself and how I felled about me. I had put myself in a hard-back shell and forgot me. I was lost to who I was. I had a one on one with Ronda I told her my trouble's, how I wanted to just end my life and what happen to me that put me in this state of mine. I've been hurt so much for so long, I didn't know how to get out. At this time, I was given a List of things to think about. I was asking to list a full thing I wanted to see in a good Man, my Glosses for my life. My list consisted of Respect for me, love me, trusted me, be independence take responsibility for myself. I will find a job, get my own place and live my own life my way. Work on my GED and LPM. I wanted to learn line dancing and I will lose weight and get all new clothes, to look like 1 million bucks.

I'm starting to love who I had become, I wanted and will be a better person. I knower I should have stay here a bit longer,

Was when I came here 21 days at this place and going to Church, I feel like a new me. I met other girls there who were like me, they had problems too. I went to church with everyone here and one morning up there and ask for Prays. Sunday evening, I said I'm going home, Monday morning I was on my way home. I went to visit Lou's. Then I went out to my bothers. Soon Lee and the kids find out I was home, I was staying in the bus he had it cleaned up for me because he know I was coming. Lee kept calling me and bothering me I was living in the bus Lynn came over every day bring letters from her dad and taking info back to her dad's. I'm afraid of being home again. Put I'm tired of running, I like to stay around and see my new grandkids. But they want to leave me alone here. I went out to the actions on Saturday night, the kids are already telling lies on me. Now I back at the crises center and seeing counselors again. Lee got a gun he is carrying with him and is looking to shot me, the cobs are so post to keep him away from me. The cops didn't believe me. I got a protection order form Lee, he not to be around me.

I did get my own apartment and I move in a 3 room and Bath. All utile pay. Everything is now going my way short after that I got a job with this nursing home I sold thing to get the money to pay my 1st weeks rent. Lou and I was very busy finding thing I needed, by this time I had a Home, Job, and my Car. Lee found out about my new place and kept coming over to see me, bring flowers and candy, cards. He was violating my protection order I had got for him to leave me alone.

He wanted to move in, but I was not ready for that yet, I didn't want to live with him. So, I said no you are not moving in here I need time to myself. After a full month when by I was happy with what I had accomplish. It was coming July of 94 I did talk to him about moving in with me, but he had a job working and making good money. So, I thought he would help me with the bills, he did pay to have the cable put in my home. He got me a sofa and dresser for the home. Short after he quit his Job and all he wanted to do was follow me around to see what I was doing. Lou and I was going to the grocer's store S&S, Lee was going to work for his last pay. He came by ware I worked to see if my car was there he's following me again. I wanted to go have a drink and just get drunk. He knows when I'm drunk cause I want to have sex. My feeling for him are not good ones, I don't know how to explain this, I do know this not LOVE.

He did find another job part time and was helping me with bills.

Our Anniversary was coming up he wanted to go out to eat, I wanted to dress up to him I look like a hoe Because that how he sees me, so I dress the part for our 26 years. I wore a red dress low cut and short, red bow in my hair and high heels Make up to match. I got to a mist I liked that part. That how he saw me.

We went to the restaurant to eat, men were looking, I don't know if Lee notice, but I didn't care. I engaged and played my part he wanted to go to the bar after lunch for a full drink after shopping got anything I wanted there so I got a high price perfume White Demine and an outfit to wear. The night was about over we went home and went to bed, he was hoping for sex, but I wasn't so it didn't happen.

Life here went on and the kids all kept getting in to trouble, Lynn and her kids was in Jail for shop lifting at shopping malls. We had to go get the baby's form, so we had the kids for the week end 18-month-old got stilling with their mother. We broth the kids home with use then started taking their baby carry all apart. We found ring watches sock, everything you name it was there.

Lee would come to my home and Take anything she could get a dollar out. She took my rent money and my rent was due. $250.

Sam got in to trouble and went to Jail all the kids was mad that me because I didn't get him out of jail. I couldn't I didn't have the money to bail them out. My kids did nothing to help me when I needed them. The only reason they were talking to me then or came around was for their dad not me. The kids cause me more trouble thought years I don't feel I owe my kids anything. Lee is still staying with me and buying me everything I want. I'm still drinking too much as before. I go to Bars myself to talk to other people there, by this time I end up drunk. There 1 to 2 men sitting with me. I was not doing anything, but Lee thought I wanted them if they talked to me. He's always come looking for me at Bars and wanting to fight someone. My days of work he wants to follow me, he thinks I'm going to do something that he wants to find out.

Times are going by and Lee is helping me with the bills I called in a lot at work because I was sick form drinking too much the night before. So, I'm not getting mush of a pay check. Lee went together on Christmas to the kids and grandkids and I had a good time we took gifts to all them.

I was part of life at last and in the moment of the excitement, I discovered Alcohol. I was very lonely, tared and I turn to drinking for comforted. 1989 I started to drink for the fun of it. Every time I would pass a Bur I had to stop in and have one, but it didn't stop at one.

I want to take NA. classes and get a good job. The drive for success was on! I'd wanted to prove to everyone my family that I could do it. We had very little money, being the only one working. Alcoholic that I was I pass the course. How I did not know my higher power had to be there. Drinking was taking over the portent part of my life. I made a lot of drinking friends there was many unhappy seems in my attornment. after I got that job I wanted so bad to work in the nursing home caring for the elderly. I was drinking called in a lot I went to work with a hangover. I work like this for 3 years in July I got sick at work my chest was hurting bad. I was having trouble lifting the people. I was losing my balance and afraid of dropping one of them. After that they sent me to the hospital in July 95. I was of work for 2 weeks and they told me not to come back So I lost my job.

Drinking did take over my life I had no control over me at all. I know this had to stop my health is getting bad because of it. I kept telling myself I can never take another drink. I always went back out and did it again. I tried to get sober in 94 and 95 went to the AA rooms, then I went back out.

New Year's Eve all the family went out to eat and their men, and Lee and me. We wanted to go out to this club on cook's hill rd. We drink and drink, but we could not get drunk there. I think it was because we eat before we went out, but we still had a good time. We had kraut and pork ribs that night to.

We moved from my 3-room place to a bigger place on 7th. Street. There where Lynn moved in with us.

Lynn had lost her kids due to not taking care of them. She was staying at a camp grounds where someone tuned her in for leaving the kids there alone, so she could go drinking. One day she was due in court to see if she was able to take care of then we had it big house on 7th. Street, we fixed up the front room for her and the 3 kids. The child service had to come see that she had a place to take then, and we both told her If we help you get these kids You are taking care of them won't. We are proving you a place to home them not a baby sitter.

Then one day me and Lee went to go fishing and she call the cops on us said we wasn't home taking care of the kids. After that I told her the kids can go back to the child service center and they did. They weren't my kids and I'm not caring for them. I saw this as a control sort on hers and Lee part.

Things are looking up for all of us, I'm working every day to keep my bills payed up. Lee was laying around the house seems Nov. 94. He said there nothing he can do as cold as it was. Now I'm working overtime to make ends meet. To keep thing going around the house and pay the bills. I was getting tired of being the only one working here. I feel I'm back was I started years ago. it is what I were trying to get away form. I worked to stay away from my home.

Coming up Dec. we dah a troubled Christmas that year we didn't go to the kids or get them gifts. We didn't have the extra money.

I was still working, and I told myself I wasn't going to drink only on my week ends of. So, Lou and I would go Fishing a lot at the Lake and take a 12 pack of beer and that's all we had. We did this all most the Summer. Oct. my birthday party I went on a binge and got so drunk, Sick, Monday morning. I had alcohol poring Lynn and shrilly said I got sick in the car and they put me to bed. I got up went in to the kitchen to get a bit it eats but I didn't make it I fell hitting my head and pass out. Lynn found me and put me back in bed, I didn't go to the doctor.

Jan. new year eve begins for me I was Sober and going to the aa meeting and the dance at the Light house Lee went out to the bars with Lou I got sick and went home early. went to bed must have been 10;pm, Lee come home early to around 11;30 he had been drinking. He set up and watch tv for a while, I went on to sleep. I'm not working now, he finely got a job we were behind on the bills. I'm still walking Lee where I needed to go. Lee had two cars and using my tags on one of them. I stay there with him for a while until my tax check came in, I made $640. So, I want out and got me a car in March.

I rented a storage room again put my things away this is my 2nd time I move out. I went and move to Lou's until I could get thing going for me. I got a job, was working then

I rented a room Lou was separate from her husband at the time. I'm still Sober Lee accused me of seeing someone at the AA meeting, when I got sober. I am working well and have my own place to live.

I move to Massively had a job there in a dairy queen, cook and waitress, I lived across form my work, so I can walk there. I was back to drinking again. My job was getting less and less no hours couldn't pay my rent, just barely making it.

What got me back to drinking again Lou? We went out to go fishing she got a case of beer and I got a 6 pack for me. Lou always said you are not an alcohol if you can stop drinking so easy. I wanted to find out for myself. we were fishing but wasn't catching anything, but we were running out of beer. We packed everything up and went in town, then to every Bar in town got drunk. I stayed at Lou's that night Lee came over the next day to see me.

I got my own place in town again I was living in a 2-room house on 4th. Street. Lee know where I was living and kept Stoking me and watching my every move. We were separated at this time, what I did was my business not his.

I started to go to the bars out at Massively, I went to Bar for drinking by myself. There was this good-looking man there drinking at the bar by himself he looked over to me and waved at me. He came over to me ask if I would like to dance with him. We went back to the table I was sitting, and he started to talk. He wanted to know why I was alone in here drinking, then I told him of my fear of Men. Then he told me about him and He was very understanding he seem to know what I was saying he was patience with me. We both drinking, he took me home. A friend took my car home with her. He took me to a motel that night we were up all night just talking about our self. Jerk brought out of me in one night what Lee couldn't do in 27 years of marriage. Jerk relayed love me I could feel the bond we had, we went to living together for about 3 months until he wanted to just want to be friends. He quit making love to me. Jerk moved out of my place because of Lee.

I didn't see Jerk for a while after that. It seems he went back to his wife.

I moved in with Lee I had nowhere else to go so I lived with him for a while.

It seems this keeps happing I don't want to be with him but, yet we keep ending up together.

Jan., I went out to get another Job I worked 10 days in a factory, it was good money my 1st. check was $300. Dollars, so I wanted to try again on my own I got a room on 2nd. Street, Lee had to move any way because he wasn't paying is bills. I was at the room for 3 months, I went back to the rooms of AA meeting I was wanting to be Sober put something kept pulling me the other way.

I moved again to a 3 room and basement home on Sugar street. It was mine. I played the deposit and the owner said go ahead and move in, pay the rent on Feb. 1 so I did I wanted this place for myself. But It didn't work this way. Come Feb. 1 we were still living together, he was back to working and I was working little jobs off and on to help with the bills. I wasn't making a lot, but it was length to pay a full bill. Then Lee got homeless again wanted to move in with me he said I'm working now than I said for how long.

The moral of this story doesn't keep going back to where you wanted out of. Call it quits and move on. don't do what I did. Run. By life is a MASS. Because of my XXX. Lee

4

LETTERS I WROTE TO HIM

I'm depressed, distrust, unhappy, every time I leave you and come back you always promise to change to control your Jealousy, you're always accusing me. We are Arguing most of the time I can never do anything right. Can't sleep with you because I'm Afraid of you or what you will do if I talk in my sleep. You get mad because I won't have SEX with you, I can't because I don't love you like I did before. I still think about the pass a lot I'm having trouble getting pass it. I believe that when I started to fall out of love with you. A lot has happened since then. You have never trusted me form the day we got married.

I'm sorry you feel this way but if you feel you need to move on with your life. I will not hold you up It up to you. I said Where are you going to live, I can't tell you think will be different if you come home. You decide what you are going to do let me, or my case manage up here know. I will come and put my thing in storage.

I have a room in the hospital I'm not a well I'm a sick person. You can pack up my thing you want me to have.

Lee I'm going to forgive you for thing you have done to me and my love one's lot of bad feeling have pass between us. I'm sorry for everything have put you thought my love. For you is long pass gone you say you don't remember what thing you have did to me Look back at what you put Lynn thought. I think you need to ask GOD to forgive you that hurt is still there. I can forgive what happen. I'm now learning to let go of bad feeling and letting go of you ask onetime if we were going to make it this time. it still a ??. I'm new working the program.

5

LETTERS HE WROTE ME

Most of what he had to say was how much he loved me and missed me, he went on saying the grandkids was missing me put I very rarely went out there. He says he can sleep he worried about me, say his heart is hurting. he says he has no life without me. he went to the doctor for Neves bills but as I know him he'll take any one's bills. He said I "didn't want to lose you I'm hurting a lot." I try to work put I can't keep you of my mine. He goes on to say I will love you till the day I dies no one will take your place. he said I wouldn't hurt you for the world, but he did hurt me he say I'm hurting my family and him. He wanted to know why I hated him so much, he denies all the thing he has done to hurt me and go on saying you know I didn't do anything. He got me a book I wanted and said he'll pay for it. He tried to find out where the safe house I was staying at. He went on saying everyone missed me and said my bother didn't because he knows where I was. That sum it up on his letters just that he's not the Blame for my problems and how I'm hurting all my family.

6 & 7

HOW I BECAME AN ALCOHOL AND HOW I OVERCAME BEING ME.

Polly Program help me. as you will read I learned.

I was part of a life that was accused, lonely, degrading, and most of all sad. I would drink to drown myself and forget why I was and who I was. Living life Like this always moving losing jobs because your husband can't trust or want. Being always watched where you go who you talk to, is very degrading, and downing me. Being belittled by someone who said they Love you, no way I don't call that love. I call that controlling by other people in my life. Not form just one but form all my family members. That include my kids who took their dads side over mine. I explement of a life time of disappointment. 33 years of my life was Robed.

The remorse Honor and Hopelessness of the next day, Courage to do battle my brain is unmanageable. Thought of doing myself in had come up all section of this as well as many political, economic, school, social, and religions back ground are people who normally mix. Among use fellow ship a friendship with understanding which is wonderful. The fact for every one of us is that we have discovered a Solution AA books Carrie those massages to suffering Alcoholics like me. Its and illness a human sickness, like a person with cancer you feel sorry and hurt for them. Put and Alcoholics stands alone with nobody to care what happens to them. There life's touch your life it brings mis sunder standing, fierce resentment, financial, insecurity, disgusted friends, and employment the list go on. I found it hard impossible to persuade an alcoholic, to discuss my situation. I tried before to talk to people of my problems but got no reply.

Now I'm in a recovery house for treatment, I feel that will elimination of my drinking, but it is just a bringing for me. The impotent detonation of my principles and my respective home my occupation, and affairs, I keep on the way I'm going there is little doubt that mush good will come. I know I can recover form it I have the opportunity and will.

I'm a Graceful for this program and would suggest to all my friends and others in need of help. As an x problem drinker, I depend upon our constant thought of others, how we may help each other. We are recovering from a hopeless condition of mine and body. I'm an Alcoholic who wants to get better over it illness, my will power is or was weak my doctor told me that I needed to quit drinking. It is tearing up my body, so I have a strong reason to quit, my health, love for myself, and changes. I'm often perfectly, sensible and well balanced except with liquor. I often possess special abilities, skills and amplitude. I could had afforded it I may had canceled Bess the house. There have been days that I could not take it and go out and do it again. My main problem is my mind and body, I have headaches, beat myself up.

I was having been willing to admit I was an Alcohols, I enjoyed my drinking pursue it into the gate of insanity or death of me. I learned that I had to fully concede to my inner most self that I was an alcoholic. My 1st. sept to recover me form Alcohol, who had lost my ability to control my drinking. I know I would not recovered completely there are no such thing as a normal drinker. I had to be honest with myself about it. Early in my drinking Career I know I could not stop drinking without help. I didn't have the desire to while I had time I was Nervous afraid of People Places and Thing.

I got sober for me going places having fun doing thing I wanted to do, it was upsetting to my family. I took myself to the rooms of AA meeting.

I went back out there started drinking again.

Jan. to July. I went on a fishing trip with my sister n law, she took beer and I got drunk, then we went Bar hopping I felled angry worried and depression. I was unable to stop drinking. I need help I was interested and conceded that I had the symptoms. I had convinced myself I had to stop, I had no excuse for drinking. Possible for me to drink again I know when I went back out I would get sick If I be honestly wanted to fine you cannot quit entirely. I had little control over the amount I took in drinking the one who feel the pain here was me not Lou, she kept saying you don't have a problem with drinking.

I know she was wrong about what I felled atheist, egoistic such an experience seems impossible but to continue as I'm meant disaster. I was tired of avoiding this issue I was having against hope. alcoholics was mere code of morals or better philosophy of life were sufficient to overcome it. lack of my will power was my dilemma. I had to find my Higher power greater then myself will solve my problem.

That meant I will have whiten the book which I believed to be spiritual as well doubtful, and PR justice. I was weak, now I believe and willing in myself. Besides a seeming inability to accept much of faith I then found me, handicap by obstinacy, sensitiveness, unreasoning. For me this kind of thinking had to stop if I was going to make it. alcohol was a great persuader it finally beat me into a state of reasonableness, readers will still ask WHY.

I had Failed to follow the past I could not recover because I didn't give it my all. Working the program, I wasn't honest with myself. I felt I was at fault, I'm naturally in incapable of grasping and developing a manner of living with rigorous honesty. I suffered from grave emotional and mental disorder, my stories disclose in general way I use to be like, what happened and what I'm like now. I wanted what most people had and was going to any length to get it I know I'm powerless over drinking, and my life a complete mass. To some this up I'm glad I find the help I need, put it didn't end there I did go back out drinking and got 2 DUI, 99 and went to jail that was no fun trip. Lost Jobs I got was homeless for a while. After all this I wanted to find help. I dated a full man who drink to like me and that all they want someone to drive for them, cook and clean more less a Slave worker is how I felt. Yes, I lived with some of these men one beat me. I met at the Bar. Some of them moved in with me. Lou and Lee came got me in Ky.

2002 on my sober date I was still working at nursing home in the Kitchen live at liberty str. Chillicothe, met Boyfriend at a dance Feb. and march he wanted me to move in with him to Adelphi Apr. 17 I lost my job, my feeling no job and no income and no place to live. put still sober. 4 29 I was moving back to Chillicothe 5,10 got me a room on 2nt str. $140 month. Got a new job working 6am to 2;30pm. about 3 weeks I got employment $204 For month, I had my sen.8 working for me with no job at this time. but I had money saved up. June, I got another apt. 126 e.4th. str. here I am paying only $133. Month. I got my unemployment check every 2 weeks for 6month. July, I got another job, part time cleaning a store room. Oct. A friend needed a place to go and I let him come stay with me. He took me out to eat for my birthday. Then he got his own place. Nov. then friend move here with me. He had lost his place. He stayed with me for 9 years. And move around to where my work was.

Thought all this I'm still sober. Jan.23 2001.

My living places and jobs working place change I was able to work jobs for 5 years at a time and live in a house for 8 years, and pay my bills with sec. 8 program yes thing look up for me I had quit drinking, quit going around thought who did, my love one finally got it and know I meant it Lee quit bothering me he got the massage to. I'm now working on my crafts now something I wanted to do for some time, making Mural and quits among other thing. Thank you, GOD for my life.

2001 I find that help and got me the best sponsor and work the program with her I got it this time. I'm sober now 18, years and living a life of happiness I'm hole now.

I hope you all get something from this book and learn from my mistakes don't let life take you there.

To sum this up is my life was hard
to live, But I live to tell it,

Just know This you will find and marry
the same as your dad and mom.

I had 25 Job's and moved 35 times.

We are now divorce seen 98 and he
still thinks he controls my life.

(But I'm not letting Him.)

I will work on book 2 of Growing up.

ABOUT THE AUTHOR

I independent and resourceful nature has been a guiding force for you throughout your life.

I have always been making decisions on your own, planning your future and helping others.

I tend to think about every small detail before you make plans, and that can sometimes make people think that you are a little negative.

Try to relax sometimes and get out of your comfort zone. It could really improve our life!

I love Writing small Story's That helps other people I'm and older gal who look that life the old school way.

I do have 4 kids and lots of grand kids as you will read in the Book and My life was a kind of not good, but I'm not a Quiter and I don't give up. on my Dreams. I have al way wanted to help the Homeless put I yet have not got there yet.

Printed in the United States
By Bookmasters

Printed in the United States
By Bookmasters